*the* JOY *of*

# MARRIAGE
## *God's* WAY

# *the* JOY *of* MARRIAGE *God's* WAY

MARRIAGE-BUILDING MESSAGES *featuring*

## BEVERLY LAHAYE,

### JULIE CLINTON, JOYCE PENNER, BARBARA ROSBERG, DEB LAASER, CARRIE OLIVER *and* LAURIE S. HALL

INTEGRITY®
PUBLISHERS
*Nashville*

**The Joy of Marriage God's Way**

Published by Integrity Publishers, a division of Integrity Media, Inc., 5250 Virginia Way, Suite 110, Brentwood, TN 37027 in association with American Association of Christian Counselors.

HELPING PEOPLE WORLDWIDE EXPERIENCE *the* MANIFEST PRESENCE *of* GOD.

Published in association with Yates and Yates, LLP, Literary Agents, Orange, California.

Unless otherwise indicated, Scripture quotations are taken from the Holy Bible, New International Version. Copyright © 1973, 1978, 1984 International Bible Society. Used by permission of Zondervan Bible Publishers.

Other Scripture references are from the following sources:

The New King James Version (NKJV), © copyright 1979, 1980, 1982, Thomas Nelson, Inc., Publishers. New American Standard Bible (NASB), © copyright 1960, 1977 by the Lockman Foundation. The Amplified Bible (AMP), © copyright 1987, The Zondervan Corporation and the Lockman Foundation. The Holy Bible, New Living Translation (NLT), copyright © 1996. Used by permission of Tyndale House Publishers, Inc., Wheaton, Illinois. All rights reserved.

ISBN 1-59145-056-X

*Printed in the United States of America*
03 04 05 06 07 08 RRD 9 8 7 6 5 4 3 2 1

# Contents

# Acknowledgments

The publishers wish to thank Tim Clinton and
Doris Rikkers for their creative and editorial
contributions to this project.

# Introduction

*May the Lord make your love increase*
*and overflow for each other.*
—1 THESSALONIANS 3:12

What a wonderful blessing that is for marriage! No matter what stage of married life we're currently in—newlywed, five years with children, fifteen years with teens, empty nesters, or golden years—we all want our marriages to be the way God created them: filled with love, understanding, and passion.

Being human, our marriages are not always as perfect as

that first union created by God in the Garden of Eden. There are times when hurt, betrayal, and distance can invade our homes and damage the relationship we have with our spouse. Although there may still be love, there is something lacking, and we know it. But there is hope. There is always help and healing available from God, the restorer of love and life. God wants us to enjoy our marriage and our mate. He wants us to feel the joy of having a special person in our life, a soul mate who will love us, care for us, and appreciate us. It was His idea that we should not go through life alone and that the union of marriage would make us stronger in life to do His will. For any marriage to be strong, we need to have God at the center as our anchor and our guide.

Whether your marriage is soaring high, cruising along comfortably, or plunging into a pit, we invite you to read these chapters and discover ways to overcome any hurts, restore your relationship, and turn the mediocre into sensational. God gave us marriage to help and support us. If we do marriage His way we will experience true joy in our relationship.

# The Joy of
# Marriage God's Way

# The Joy of Marriage God's Way

BEVERLY LAHAYE

*Be encouraged in heart and united in love.*

—COLOSSIANS 2:2

I don't know about you but I'm always excited about receiving a wedding invitation. The thought of a wedding makes the romantic in me come out. I think it does for a lot of women. Starting in about January of each year every town and city across America starts focusing on the upcoming "wedding season"—May through August. Florists, bridal shops, and caterers are in a flurry over the hectic pace that the wedding season brings. Brides are inundated with endless ideas of what dresses to wear, what tuxedos to rent, the flowers . . . the cake . . . the music . . . the bridal registries, and on and on and on.

The glamorization of weddings and the appeal to the romantic in every woman is at an all-time high. Daytime television is loaded with soap opera wedding events, prime-time TV features at least one or two "finales" of the season's show with a wedding, and a cable station has a regular feature called *A Wedding Story.* But have you noticed what they all have in common? They all focus on the pomp and glitter—a glamorous parade with a few words spoken by the smiling groom and the radiant bride. There's no mention of this being a sacred event—one ordained and created by God. Everyone is more worried about the dress, the flowers, the food; and the sacredness of the moment is lost.

The world has commercialized, romanticized, and trivialized this sacred union to the point that many women, and men, have forgotten the true purpose of marriage. By the time the last piece of wedding cake is consumed and the thank-you notes written, the honeymoon is long over and so is the marriage. A marriage based on the wedding event, the party atmosphere, and "the biggest day of your life" has a weak foundation—a worldly foundation that will not withstand the strains and the challenges of a lifetime. But a marriage that has God as its foundation—a marriage God's way—is a marriage that will endure "till death do us part."

Exactly what is a marriage God's way? What does God really want your marriage to be like?

## GOD WANTS YOUR MARRIAGE TO BE SACRED

Marriage was the first institution created and blessed by God. It started in the Garden of Eden with Adam and Eve. God first of all created Eve because "it is not good for man to be alone" (Genesis 2:18). God recognized that Adam needed a companion, "a helper," to keep him company. Nothing God had created up to that point—birds, animals, reptiles, or the beautiful surroundings—filled that void in man. So God made humans in need of companionship. Now we also know that God made man in his own image. Genesis 1:27 says, "So God created man in his own image, in the image of God he created him; male and female he created them." He made man, He made woman, He made them unique, and He creatively crafted every sexual part of them. "And it was very good" (Genesis 1:31).

God then blessed Adam and Eve (Genesis 1:28) and gave out His very first command, "Be fruitful and multiply." Well, friends, there's only one way to do that—by having sexual relations. So now we know that God created male and female, blessed them, and told them to have sex. And note the timing. All of this happens *before* Satan shows up, tempts Eve, and entices her to disobey God. All of this happens and God declares it "very good." Male and female and all their sexual drives, desires, and body parts are sacred to God; they are special and designed just as He wanted them to be in a perfect world. Originally there was nothing "dirty" about sex in marriage—it was pure and purposeful. It was designed to eliminate loneliness, to provide security and happiness, and to provide the most intimate expression of our love for our spouse. No shame and guilt here. And even though the world has tainted sex and turned it into a money-making commercial entity, Christians should approach it otherwise—as a sacred and blessed gift from God.

In the New Testament Jesus shows His approval for the institution of marriage by showing up at a wedding and performing His first-ever miracle. Later He talks about marriage and says, "Haven't you read that at the beginning the Creator 'made them male and female,' and said, 'For this reason a man will leave his father and mother and be united to his wife, and the two will become one flesh'? So they are no longer two, but one. Therefore what God has joined together, let man not separate'" (Matthew 19:4–6).

The apostle Paul, through the Holy Spirit's inspiration, also has this to say about marriage: "Marriage should be honored by all, and the marriage bed kept pure" (Hebrews 13:4). The purpose for keeping your marriage bed pure is simple —it's a sacred thing, and throughout the Bible God's commands are very clear on how to handle sacred things: with care and respect.

Another aspect of the sacredness of marriage is its private nature. Marriage is the ultimate relationship between husband and wife. That doesn't mean you can ignore other relationships: There are extended family relationships and friends you do have to take into consideration in a marriage, but when the day ends and the bedroom door closes, marriage is about two people and two people only. I get really nervous at weddings when the bride and groom go on and on with highly personal pledges and promises at the public ceremony when they should remain private. Marriage is sacred, or private between the two of you and God. There are some promises that need to be public; there are other things that are best shared just between the two of you. What goes on in the bedroom and in the intimate moments of your married life should not be shared or discussed casually with others. Keep your marriage sacred. Keeping certain aspects of it private will add to your intimacy and your closeness because you'll know that only the two of you know and share certain secrets.

## GOD WANTS TO BE PART OF YOUR MARRIAGE

Marriage is very close to God's heart. It is so dear to Him that He uses marriage to describe Christ's love for the church (Ephesians 5:22–33). He created marriage, He instituted marriage, and He wants to bless your marriage and be part of it to ensure its joy and success. And this goes way beyond just inserting the phrase "before God and these witnesses" into the wedding ceremony. That phrase is included more out of tradition than for its actual meaning or purpose. Consciously review the words of your ceremony and the words of the songs to be sung at the wedding, and be absolutely certain that your special day will be a witness to all those in attendance that your union is of God, and He is at the center of your relationship.

Your wedding vows are pledged in the sight of God and should not be taken lightly. Ecclesiastes 5:4–5 says, "When you make a vow to God, do not delay in fulfilling it. He has no pleasure in fools; fulfill your vow. It is better not to vow than to make a vow and not fulfill it." Your vow made to your marriage partner is also being made to God.

Marital strength involves God. The Bible says, "Be strong in the Lord and in his mighty power" (Ephesians 6:10). When you involve God in your marriage, you create a bond that cannot break. It may sway in hurricane force winds when life is stormy, but it will not be crushed. It may get pounded by adversity and pain, but it will not be destroyed—not if you have God's strength and His mighty power as the foundation of your relationship.

## GOD WANTS YOUR MARRIAGE TO BE PASSIONATE

God created you as a sexual being. He intended man and woman to be different but at the same time to complement each other and to be "united as one flesh." God created the passions and desires in the human race as a good thing. Sexual desire was created for our mutual pleasure and enjoyment and "it was very good." Unfortunately the positive aspects and the positive teachings in the Bible about sex and marriage pale in the shadow of the numerous warnings, commandments, and admonishments against fornication, adultery, and prostitution. Generations of young people have been preached at with wagging fingers and the "do nots" to the point that most of us grew up thinking there was something dark, forbidden, and downright wrong with desiring sex and enjoying it once we got married. But here's the good news, if you haven't heard: God created passion and He wants you as a married couple in the sacred marriage bed to enjoy it. It is just not true that anything that can be called spiritually acceptable or sacred cannot be enjoyed. God created sex to be sacred, to be the utmost in commitment and relationship between two people, but He created it good and fun and enjoyable. God made every one of our human drives and our physical and emotional makeup in such a way that it could be used for our enjoyment, not for our personal torture. Our God is a God of love, not a God of torment, teasing, and torture. He gave us the gift of sexuality for a specific and pleasurable activity.

Early in Genesis, after God finished creating male and female in His own image, He blessed them and then gave them a command. This was the very first "to do" in the Bible and it's a positive and pleasurable command: "Be fruitful and multiply." Now, as you already know, there is only one natural way to do this: by having sex. Of course it also implies that sex has the purpose of procreation, but for most people, not every encounter results in conception. There's a lot of pleasure going on while trying to fulfill God's command. Many couples are physically unable to conceive a child, but that does not mean they have to stop making love.

Many years ago my husband Tim and I wrote a book called *The Act of Marriage,* which discusses how the Bible supports the fact that God approves of lovemaking between married partners:

Genesis 2 affords a more detailed description of God's creation of Adam and Eve, including the statement that God Himself brought Eve to Adam (Genesis 2:22), evidently to introduce them formally and give them the command to be fruitful. Then it beautifully describes their innocence in these words: "The man and his wife were both naked, and they felt no shame" (Genesis 2:25). Adam and Eve knew no embarrassment or shame on that occasion for three reasons: 1) they were introduced by a holy and righteous God who commanded them to make love; 2) their minds were not preconditioned to guilt, for no prohibitions concerning the act of marriage had yet been given; 3) and no other people were around to observe their intimate relations.

God acknowledges the passionate needs of a husband and wife by giving a command that is included in the laws of

Moses. It's one law from God that most newlyweds would love to have enforced today: "If a man has recently married, he must not be sent to war or have any other duty laid on him. For one year he is to be free to stay at home and bring happiness to the wife he has married" (Deuteronomy 24:5). Wow! Wouldn't that be fun—to have your mate told that his only duty for one year was to make you happy! If we even mentioned the concept today, someone would exclaim, "In your dreams!" Even though our society wouldn't accommodate this arrangement, the command shows us that God intended marriages to be for the mutual happiness of both men and women, and that that first year of marriage, especially, is a time of great affection and passion as the couple gets to know and enjoy one another.

There are other passages in the Bible that clearly affirm God's intention for sex in marriage. The entire Book of Song of Solomon is a beautiful, sensuous dialogue between two young lovers shortly after their marriage. "I found the one my heart loves. I held him and would not let him go" (Song of Songs 3:4). To first-time readers of this booklong poem, it's a bit disconcerting that God would allow such frank and passionate sentences to be included in the Bible. And yet this book of the Bible, like all the others, is inspired and "God breathed" (2 Timothy 3:16). It has been included in every edition of the Bible since the very first printing. There has never been a debate that it was too graphic or too descriptive and should be dropped or entered into "adult only" editions. No, God intended for us to have a healthy and positive view of sex in marriage and with this book of His Word, He proves it.

But the critical passage in the Bible about marital love is found in Paul's letter to the Corinthians:

> Each man should have his own wife, and each woman her own husband. The husband should fulfill his marital duty to his wife, and likewise the wife to her husband. The wife's body does not belong to her alone but also to her husband. In the same way, the husband's body does not belong to him alone but also to his wife. Do not deprive each other except by mutual consent and for a time, so that you may devote yourselves to prayer. Then come together again so that Satan will not tempt you

because of your lack of self-control. (1 Corinthians 7:2–5)

Sex is not for power or persuasion or for using your spouse. It is for your mutual pleasure, and for selfless giving, and for intimately expressing your deep love for your mate.

## GOD WANTS YOU TO BE BEST FRIENDS

A marriage based on friendship is one that has the strength and the power to endure. Passion is important, but friendship is strong stuff. Friendship creates a firm security that makes just being together renew your spirit. It's the place in marriage that's like a warm blanket on a cold winter night—a place of serenity, peace, calm, and joy. Marriage to your very best friend is the deepest of friendships. You can share everything in confidence, talk endlessly about your dreams, and care deeply for each other. In fact,

> *A marriage based on friendship is one that has the strength and the power to endure.*

your sharing continues even when words are not spoken—your spouse's mere presence is your peace.

I love the biblical statement: "This is my lover, this my friend" (Song of Songs 5:16). It says it all. This is the best friend you'll ever have; you'll share more with this person than with any other friend you have in a lifetime. You share your life, your future, and your body with this very special friend.

Marriage is the ultimate in friendship; it has all the qualities of a good friendship and then some. Good friendships are a give-and-take proposition; marriage is even more so. Other key qualities of friendship include the following: friends can say almost anything to one another, friends are confidants and keep certain things confidential, friends counsel and advise one another, friends listen, friends make sacrifices for the other person, they have no hidden agendas, they can always be counted on, they have fun together, and friends overlook the small stuff.

Good friendships are never selfish. The apostle Paul told the Philippians, "Each of you should look not only to your own interests, but also to the interests of others" (Philippians 2:4). This is great advice for a marriage relationship as well.

Unselfish love is putting the needs of your spouse first. Genuine love flourishes in giving. Robert Moeller in his book *To Have and to Hold* prefers to call it "giving love" rather than "making love": "Making love sounds too much like the mere mechanical joining of a male and female body. Giving love sounds much more like the sharing of your soul, your affection, your respect, your deepest concern, and your heart with another person." The best sex is the mutual giving of our body to our spouse—nobody should be *making* anyone have sex; that's selfish and using the other person for your personal gratification and purpose. But when you *give* love, you're concentrating on the other person's pleasure and enjoyment; you're loving your spouse, not using him or her.

Another aspect of friendship in marriage is "a friend loves at all times" (Proverbs 17:17). This type of love goes the distance. It endures through a bout with the flu, through ten checks that bounce at the bank, through the car that won't start on a Monday morning, through conflicts with parents, and through disagreements over how to squeeze the toothpaste tube. Through all that, friends love. Friendship is the bricks of a marriage—passionate sex is the cement.

## GOD WANTS YOUR MARRIAGE TO BE FUN

Marriage is definitely serious business, not to be taken lightly or to be thought of as temporary or just until the romance fades. But God wants you also to have fun. Marriage is a relationship with the person who means more to you than any other relationship you will ever have. This person is your soul mate who knows and cares about you better than anyone (even your mother). So be joyful, be playful. There's an old song that says, "Accentuate the positive, eliminate the negative." Do that. When life is good, enjoy it. Learn to be content with what you have and live in the moment. Don't misunderstand me, you need to have dreams and make plans for your future, and God has promised us a great future (Jeremiah 29:11), but be sure you enjoy getting there. Too many couples get so wrapped up in what will be that they miss the fun they can have along the way. Most of the fun is in achieving your dreams.

When you laugh, laugh together. Laughter with each other and at what's happening in life will get you through a lot. Never have fun at your partner's expense. Be sensitive to each other's needs and "sore spots." Don't make fun of the fact that he's not handy with a hammer; don't criticize her cooking; don't make fun of a weight gain. But do learn to laugh at yourself.

Try new things too: Go on an adventure, drive to a new town and see something different. In marriage you can explore each other's interests as well as your sexuality. God doesn't limit your joy—you do.

## HOW TO HAVE A MARRIAGE GOD'S WAY

1. *Study the Scripture.* Many churches today require that couples attend a series of premarital counseling sessions with the pastor who will officiate at the ceremony. During your counseling sessions be sure that you spend some time discussing God's view of marriage. Study the various Bible passages mentioned within this chapter together. Be sure that you have left preconceived notions and soap-opera/commercialized perceptions of sex behind before you begin your married life.

2. *Pray.* Learn to pray together out loud. This will keep

your marriage focused on God and each other, away from yourself. Pray for God to bless your marriage. Pray for wisdom and guidance. Pray for joy and the ability to realize when life is good and to be content. Pray for strength when you must face the difficult times in life—those times that qualify for the "for poorer, . . . in sickness" parts of your marriage vows. Pray that no matter what God sends your way, you will be drawn closer together, not apart.

Pray for the Holy Spirit to live in your lives and to fill every corner of your home, so that you can feel God's presence in every room. Jesus promised that He will be there: "For where two or three come together in my name, there am I with them" (Matthew 18:20).

3. *Make God part of your marriage ceremony.* Ask your pastor to help you make sure this focus is firm and secure and obvious on your wedding day. He may have some suggestions of how to visually incorporate your unity with God and with each other into the ceremony. Some couples braid three strands of rope together to symbolize the three-way unity they have with God in their marriage. This gesture beautifully illustrates Ecclesiastes 4:12: "A cord of three strands is

not quickly broken." With God as the third strand in your marriage, you will have enormous strength. Another passage that can illustrate your focus on God in your marriage is Joshua 24:15: "Choose for yourselves this day whom you will serve. . . . But as for me and my household, we will serve the LORD."

If you are already married and realize that you did not make an obvious commitment to God in your ceremony, take some time to recommit your marriage to God and ask him to come and be the head of your home and the center of your marriage.

4. *Keep your sex life private.* If you agree that marriage is sacred and a very special gift from God, then what you do in the bedroom (or anywhere else in the house, for that matter) is not for public announcement or discussion. You will feel more confident and closer as a couple if your sexual escapades are privileged information in the bedroom. How you mutually share your love and affection is for your enjoyment between the two of you. The mystery of shared love and affection loses its exclusiveness and thrill if broadcast in lunchrooms or discussed at the gym or over coffee.

God intended for sex to be a private matter, so keep it that way.

5. *Make your marriage a priority.* Place your marriage second on your priority list—right behind God. This isn't going to be easy, but it's very, very important in order to create a marriage "God's way." Think about this a minute: This means that your job, your hobbies, your children, your dreams, your parents, or whatever, land in the third or lesser position but your marriage should be cemented in second place. In real practical terms this means that if what you are doing causes your marriage to suffer and makes your mate miserable, you need to alter it in some way. Pleasing your mate, being attentive to him, and spending time together as a couple will bring you true joy and bind you closer together.

A marriage God's way is a marriage that lasts, a marriage that is "rooted and established in love" (Ephesians 3:17). It is the ultimate in what God created and always intended marriage and a loving relationship to be. You cannot achieve it on your own with lots of advice and endless marriage books and wedding planners; you need God's help every day and through each moment of your married life to have a pure and true and lasting love as described in 1 Corinthians 13:1–8, 13:

> If I speak in the tongues of men and of angels, but have not love, I am only a resounding gong or a clanging cymbal. If I have the gift of prophecy and can fathom all mysteries and all knowledge, and if I have a faith that can move mountains, but have not love, I am nothing. If I give all I possess to the poor and surrender my body to the flames, but have not love, I gain nothing.
>
> Love is patient, love is kind. It does not envy, it does not boast, it is not proud. It is not rude, it is not self-seeking, it is not easily angered, it keeps no record of wrongs. Love does not delight in evil but rejoices with the truth. It always protects, always trusts, always hopes, always perseveres. Love never fails. . . .
>
> And now these three remain: faith, hope and love. But the greatest of these is love.

## ABOUT THE AUTHOR

Beverly LaHaye is the founder and chairman of Concerned Women for America (CWA). She has authored eight books and co-authored seven books, both fiction and nonfiction; one of the best known is *The Act of Marriage,* written with her husband, Tim. Beverly currently serves on the boards of Liberty University, Childcare International, and the International Right to Life Federation.

## VERSES THAT INSPIRE

"For my thoughts are not your thoughts, neither are your ways my ways," declares the LORD. (Isaiah 55:8)

Teach me your way, O LORD, and I will walk in your truth; give me an undivided heart, that I may fear your name. (Psalm 86:11)

Let love and faithfulness never leave you; bind
them around your neck, write them on the tablet
of your heart. (Proverbs 3:3)

Follow the way of love. (1 Corinthians 14:1)

Blessed are all who fear the LORD, who walk in his ways.
You will eat the fruit of your labor; blessings and pros-
     perity will be yours.
Your wife will be like a fruitful vine within your house;
your sons will be like olive shoots around your table.
Thus is the man blessed who fears the LORD.
May the LORD bless you from Zion all the days of your
     life. (Psalm 128:1–5)

The LORD has done great things for us, and we are
filled with joy. (Psalm 126:3)

# Spiritual Intimacy in Marriage

JULIE CLINTON

*Though one may be overpowered, two can defend themselves.*
*A cord of three strands is not easily broken.*

—ECCLESIASTES 4:12

Most couples have a very poor spiritual life together, not just in the early stages of marriage, but throughout their lives together. But there's nothing more significant than a husband and wife coming together to embrace God and seek His face in marriage. When this happens, you will taste of the marriage you've always wanted.

## UNDERSTANDING SPIRITUAL INTIMACY

Spiritual intimacy is the act of consistently and intentionally coming together before God to know Him more intimately and to serve Him more fully and completely, or more simply, knowing and seeking God together. Unfortunately, according to author Neil Clark Warren, only 10–15 percent of couples really enjoy true spirituality. I know for Tim and me, so much seemed to compete for our spiritual affection—to rob us of the joy God intended. The desire was there, but we would get lost along the way and eventually become more discouraged. Learning the basics will help you develop a more spiritual marriage.

## THE BASICS OF SPIRITUAL INTIMACY

Have a purpose, a spiritual vision for your marriage—even if your husband doesn't. Such a vision reminds you that marriage is ordained of God. And He is the one who desires to bless your marriage. Scripture says when your ways follow after the Lord, "it will make even your enemies to be at peace with you." Our lives must be defined by John 3:30, which says, "He which is Christ must become greater and I must become less." When He is the center, it changes everything.

Knowing what spiritual intimacy is not helps too. First, spiritual intimacy *is not* about changing your spouse. While that will probably occur—changing Him is not the goal. As women we are born fixers. We like to fix everything that we think is wrong or just not perfect. But our purpose should never be to use God as a weapon or simply for the benefit of changing our husband. Not long ago I read *Lies Women Believe* by Nancy Leigh DeMoss. She mentions forty lies that women often believe. One lie is, "It is my responsibility to change my mate." Then she goes on to say:

> When we try to change our mate, the focus is off of our needs as a wife and our own personal walk with God. We can change ourselves, however, we cannot change the heart of our spouse. Only God can do that. Many Christian wives don't realize that they have two very powerful weapons available to them that are much more effective than the whining, the complaining, and the preaching that we so often

do. The first weapon is a Godly life, which God can use to create conviction and spiritual hunger in our husband. The second weapon is prayer. The wife that consistently points out things she wants her husband to change makes him defensive and resistant. If she would only take these concerns to the Lord, appeal to a higher power, to act in her husband's life, it's so hard for a man to resist God rather than to resist a nagging wife.

Second, spiritual intimacy *is not* about getting God on your side. Your main goal or purpose ought to be taking the focus off of yourself and allowing God to work in and through you to make your husband more like Him. It is not about getting God for you. The wonderful truth about letting God work in and through you is the reality that He is always for you!

I once heard someone say the word *intimacy* can be divided into three words: *Into-me-see*, which means, you're looking into my heart, you're looking at the desires of my heart. We need to learn to look into the heart of God so that when He looks into ours, He sees the heart of God in many ways.

There are two main ingredients for spiritual intimacy: safety and honesty. Since spiritual intimacy requires such deep vulnerability, I feel safety is a main issue. In your marriage, you should feel safe. Your marriage needs to be a place where you can both be yourselves—a place where you are free to express your thoughts and concerns without any fear of judgment. One thing is certain—intimacy will never rise above the level of fear in the relationship. Let me give you a little example. When Tim and I were first married, we would spend all of our summers in Montana. My parents owned two businesses and we would work all summer long so we could go back to college and have money to pay for our schooling. I can remember the very first year we were married, we tried so hard to have a spiritual, intimate life together and with my family. One of the first times we prayed together, Tim was leading us (my family) in prayer and he stumbled over his words. Very innocently, I started laughing. It was funny and kind of cute, but what a mistake at the time. I made him feel very uncomfortable. He still remembers it like it was yesterday. Of course, we laugh together about it now—but that's something you do *not* want to do in a marriage.

Honesty is the second main ingredient. You need to be willing to express your honest feelings always in love (Ephesians 4:15). You need to be able to be yourself and not to be fake. If your spouse is angry or discouraged, then it's your job to model honesty. You need to lead the way because one person can help change a marriage. We need both safety and honesty to have intimacy because if a spouse does not feel safe, he or she will not be able to be honest. The end result, then, is desire—a spiritual hunger for God together—with no substance.

## THE BARRIERS TO SPIRITUAL INTIMACY

Why is spiritual intimacy so difficult to achieve? While the list is endless, let me give a couple of the key barriers and roadblocks that prevent us from being on the spiritual intimacy track.

1. *Stress.* One of the roadblocks is the stressors of everyday life. Judith Wallerstein and Sandra Blakeslee, in their book *The Good Marriage,* say, "In today's marriages in which people work long hours, travel extensively and juggle careers

with family, more forces tug at the relationship than ever before. Modern marriages are battered by the demands of her workplace as well as his, by changing values, by anxiety about making ends meet each month, by geographical moves, by unemployment and recession, by the vicissitudes of child-care, and by a host of other issues."

When you're stressed, all your energies are on protecting yourself and solving problems that created the stress in the first place. There's little energy left to spend time with and develop a deep relationship with your spouse and with your Lord. Controlling or managing everyday stress is a problem that everyone needs to work on.

2. *Time.* We just have no time to give. If you are like me—you're saying, "Amen. Go, girl!" Richard Swensen, in his book *Margin,* states that the average couple today spends as little as four minutes a day in meaningful couple time. It's hard to balance all the demands like a job, children, and a spouse. Like my mother told me when I was a teenager, "If you don't make time now for the Lord, you will never have time later on." We need to make time with our spouse and time with God a high priority every day.

3. *Satanic Assault.* Ephesians 6:12 says, "For our struggle is not against flesh and blood, but against the rulers, against the authorities, against the powers of this dark world and against the spiritual forces of evil in the heavenly realms." We are in a spiritual warfare and our enemy is Satan. I believe Satan's key targets are your marriage and your relationship with the Lord. You may ask, "Why is that so?" I believe it is because we oversee God's sacred institution, which is the family.

4. *Selfishness.* None of us has mastered the unselfish life. No matter how much we love and are committed to our spouse, selfishness arises all too often. This only communicates to our spouse that he is alone and that he needs to take care of himself. Evil's intent has always been to get us to focus on self and to believe that God is not even there for us. Such thinking and behaving destroys our love life with God and our love life with our spouse.

5. *Traditions.* We all grow up with different ways of worshiping God. In some homes, spiritual intimacy was very important and our parents modeled that for us; in others it was not. Regardless, parental influence and traditions go

deep. Bringing together two different ways of seeking out God can be quite challenging. I feel very blessed to have been brought up in a family where my parents modeled spiritual intimacy for me. For example, at night when I passed by my parents' bedroom where their door was cracked open just a little, I would often see them praying together. They would share prayer requests, have devotions, read God's Word, and just share their thoughts—their feelings and the activities of their day. Many times I would even see them crying together. It placed a real hunger in me for that kind of relationship in marriage. Perhaps you were not blessed with that role model. Maybe your husband was brought up in family where spiritual intimacy was not modeled at all—or they were very private about it. Since it is true that families tend to reproduce themselves, you're going to have to talk this through and not just assume that your spouse understands the importance of sharing.

6. *Negative Emotions.* Fear, discouragement, anger . . . There are so many negative emotions that can be a roadblock to spiritual intimacy. I'm sure that you can name many more. I mention fear because a lot of couples are intimidated or

embarrassed to pray in front of their spouse. In addition, there may be times when you feel very discouraged about life and disconnected from God to the point that you don't think that God even cares about you. Anger is another emotional roadblock. It's so hard to pray with your spouse when you're frustrated and angry at him. Successful couples have learned to manage their anger. In and of itself, anger is not bad, but it's what we do in our anger that really matters. There are three recipients of your anger: yourself, your spouse, and the Lord. It's very hard to feel safe, be honest, laugh, or pray with someone you're angry with. That's where Paul encourages us. He says, "Be careful to do what is right. Live at peace with everyone." He also warns us, "Do not take revenge" (Romans 12:19). Your emotions signal troubled waters and a need for intimacy—but don't let them ever be barriers to God together. Acknowledge them and take each one to God.

7. *Knowledge.* Maybe one or both of you don't understand who God is and how to approach Him together. Hebrews 11:6 tells us that whoever "comes to [God] must first believe that he exists, and that he rewards those who

earnestly seek Him." Maybe you don't know how to pray or start reading the Bible. I recommend that you seek out a Bible-believing pastor, get involved in your local church, and get started in your journey.

8. *The Gender Gap.* Men and women often see things differently. Intimacy can mean one thing to the husband and another to the wife. That's why we have to connect. And we have to discuss these differences up-front. I've heard many husbands say, "I'm pretty intimate as a husband. I've really invested in our marriage. I took my wife out to eat this week. I mowed the lawn and I bathed the kids. I invest a lot of time in my wife and family." Well, according to the wife, he's far from a ten out of ten. He might be a six out of ten. Most of her needs, she feels, are not getting met. So what does she do? She continues to push him, doesn't she? Which only makes him feel more threatened, which threatens their intimacy. He thinks such behavior is demanding and controlling. On the other hand, the wife thinks, *I'm not going to settle for six out of ten. I'm not getting my needs met and that's important to me.* Rather than fight it out, we need to talk it out. Discuss your differences. Learn to connect. Remember, *into-me-see?* When

you do, you'll close that gender gap—and open the doors for spiritual intimacy.

9. *"One-upmanship" is another issue.* Inferiority and superiority have something to do with one-upmanship. Such a message destroys intimacy. Perhaps you are the one who is very spiritually in tune with the Lord. You were brought up in a Christian home, you went to Bible school, and you may even be able to read Greek and Hebrew. If so, your spouse may feel very intimidated to read God's Word and to try to apply it to life. Maybe you're overly active in the church and you hound your spouse with, "You need to do the same." You have to be very careful of the message you convey because you could come across as a know-it-all and subtly turn your spouse away from God, not toward Him. Remember, spiritual intimacy is not about impressing your spouse; it's about building a relationship with the Lord Jesus Christ together.

Another aspect of one-upmanship is the submission issue. Submission is not about being the boss or ruler. It's about responsibility—never superiority and inferiority. Sadly many men have taken an erroneous view of a godly concept.

According to Les and Leslie Parrott, "Submission or headship could best be described as being the first to honor, the first to nurture, and the first to meet your partner's needs."

No matter which of these barriers you struggle with, constantly ask yourself, "What is coming between God and me?"

## THE BUILDING BLOCKS OF SPIRITUAL INTIMACY

Spontaneous structure—sounds like an oxymoron, doesn't it—like jumbo shrimp. But knowing God involves spontaneity and structure. Becoming Christlike is not a program, and it's not a method; it's about a relationship with God. It isn't about time with God, although that is very important. It's about a relationship with Him.

So many times we want an easy twelve-step program to help make us more spiritual. How we've tried! I smile when I think of all the different things we've done to know God—devotionals, books, one-year Bibles, etc. I think sometimes we work too hard or we feel we need to in order to know God. But we need to remember that God wants to know us.

He actually pursues us. And that's what the phrase "spontaneous structure" is all about.

Spontaneity involves those unplanned moments, those special moments in your life when God just drops in. My husband Tim remembers a special moment that he had as a child. He can remember many Sunday mornings lying in bed and hearing his mother practicing the piano for church that day. She would practice those old, familiar hymns. He told me, "What a special, meaningful time that was for me to reflect on God as I heard her play and sing those old songs —she didn't just sing them; she believed them." That was a special moment that wasn't planned. It was an unplanned moment that God gave him.

I spend a lot of time traveling in the car running errands or taking the children to school or to other activities. During my drive time I usually turn on the radio. Occasionally an announcement or some special song will remind me of my need for God. At other times I'm reminded of Tim. And I'll actually stop the car and pray that God would be near him as he ministers to so many people. That's a special moment that God brings into my life. But so many times we are preoccupied and miss those special moments. People who have the gas pedal to the floor are doomed to be godless. We miss seeing the work of God, but wonderfully we have One who pursues us at any cost—in pain or beauty or rebellion—to win our hearts. That's a great God. Start looking for God around you. You might be shocked at how busy He is—especially in your life and marriage.

Besides spontaneous moments we must be focused on structured moments—those scheduled times and deliberate efforts that make up a disciplined, spiritual life. This includes Bible reading, Bible study, praise and worship, church attendance, fasting, prayer, and more. In his book *Celebration of Discipline*, Richard Foster states: "We so many times believe we have to have everything just perfect or everything just right in our life before we can start a spiritual life with the Lord. We will never be at that point, will we? So what we need to do is, he says we need to pray, we need to come to God no matter what." Probably the easiest place to start a structured spiritual like is to focus on prayer. Make room and time for God daily. He'll meet with you, and I promise your cup will overflow with joy and love.

## THE BLESSINGS OF SPIRITUAL INTIMACY

Andrew Greeley, author of *Faithful Attraction,* found that couples who actually pray together scored higher on all aspects concerning their marital happiness. Here is what several of the women from the Extraordinary Women series have shared with me on what spiritual intimacy means to them in their marriages.

> When my husband and I went into mission work my husband's job was to establish that mission all the way around the world so he was on the road for months and months on end. One year he was gone for ten months. I was a young mom raising three children so prayer brought us together. He would call me from Australia, which was literally the opposite end of the world, and say, "I miss you, honey." And I'd say, "I know you do." Although we were apart, we were together through prayer. I could go anywhere on my knees. He could too. So we were with each other and prayer was our lifeline basically. [JILL BRISCOE]

I feel very sustained because I know that Mark prays for me. I hope he feels sustained knowing that I pray for him. It's a deep blessing to me to know that today Mark is praying for me. Just last night as we said goodbye, he said, "I'm praying for you." My heart soared. I hope that I've enriched his life that way too. I probably haven't done that nearly as well as I feel like he's done that for me, but it creates such a powerful unity. [LISA MCMINN]

> *Praying together will create a spiritual intimacy in your marriage that will yield other blessings.*

Prayer has played a tremendous role as the foundation to our relationship, especially since we came to faith in Christ. As a result, we saw tremendous change just in our ability to communicate with each other. I believe prayer is the key to having an enriched marriage, to making your marriage go the distance, and to being able to grow spiritually together. [CLAUDIA ARP]

I have prayed for my husband, Garth, through the years and I know that he has prayed for me. Every time I go to speak somewhere, the last thing I say as I kiss him goodbye is, "Be sure and pray for me." And he'll say, "Okay, what time are you speaking?" That's such a reassurance to me and a powerful way to say I love you. [SANDRA D. WILSON]

My husband Gary and I experienced radical change in our lives and marriage when we began to be very serious about intimacy with Christ. Spiritual intimacy makes a big difference in your relationship. It's more than just trying to apply some techniques and some tools to make your relationship work; it allows God to provide what we need in order to make it work. Out of the process of growing spiritually, like taking time to prayer together, I noticed that Gary became a lot more intentional about taking time just to chat with me—which is very important to me. Growing closer to God brings you closer to each other. [CARRIE OLIVER]

It's important to put a little time aside, like five minutes a day to meet with God without an agenda, without your Bible, without your prayer tools, without anything. You need to just sit before the Lord. Sit quietly until your focus turns from you to Him and you begin to sense His grace. God wants to say things to you and you need to say things to Him that have nothing to do with your family, or your husband, or your ministry. God's waiting for us to wait. When we eventually get around to showing up, then we find we've got company. And that, to me, is my most precious time, that waiting time. [JILL BRISCOE]

Some women have husbands who are supportive and are really ready to pray together, others don't. If your husband's not there yet, you can start by praying for him. Or start a prayer journal. For years I've had a prayer journal. I simply jot down my prayer requests and later I'll go back and write the answers. This has helped me in so many ways to pray and feel closer both to God and to Dave. When and if your husband's ready to pray together, you can start on different levels. You can make a list together and take turns praying through that list. Or if you're not quite to that point, you can follow the quicker model and share a silent prayer together. And of course, the tradition is, you end that silent prayer with a holy kiss.

[CLAUDIA ARP]

## HELPFUL HINTS

Here are some thoughts to keep you focused.

1. *Keep the key purpose locked in your heart.* Spiritual intimacy is about knowing and seeking God—together.

2. *Get started.* Get back into church. Get back to reading the Bible, to listening to Christian music, to praying, and more. God wants to spend intimate time with you. Approach God with a spirit of expectation, just like our children approach us. They don't worry about food or clothes. They know that we love them, that we provide everything for them. Likewise, God is loving, and He wants us to come to Him believing He will fill our needs. If you're tired of trying

or are simply exhausted, be reminded of Philippians 4:13, which says, "I can do everything through [Christ] who gives me strength."

3. *Don't set yourself up for failure.* Don't expect to read an entire book of the Bible the first night of couple devotions. If your husband has never prayed with you before, don't expect him to pray for thirty minutes. Set very short-term goals and use variety. If you have never prayed together as a couple, maybe you could begin by having silent prayer in the same room. In time you might be ready to hold hands and have silent prayer. And eventually you might be able to give prayer requests to one another and take turns praying, maybe in a sentence format. After a while you'll actually be able to have a deep, meaningful prayer time together. Few moments in a marriage are as powerful as praying for and with each other.

4. *Don't be critical of what's happening in your spiritual life together as a couple.* Nothing will sap the strength out of your efforts more quickly.

5. *Most importantly, don't quit.* James 4:8 reminds us that when we draw near to God, He will draw near to us. Don't let distractions or discouragement rob you of His presence.

## MORE BLESSINGS

One blessing is that our conversation and our thought life begin to change. So many times our talk with our spouse is so superficial. It's just hard to relate one-on-one in today's fast-paced world. But if you spend time with God, I grant your thoughts and your conversation will change and deepen your intimacy. Remember, intimacy is *into-me-see*. When you put God into the center of your marriage, it will de-center both of you.

I like the illustration of the marriage triangle, with God at the top and the husband on one side and the wife on the other side. As you grow closer in love with the Lord, you will also grow closer in love with one another. You will become more one in your marriage.

Another blessing of spiritual intimacy is that it increases our relatedness. As you grow in Christ, you develop more shared values, shared directions, and shared goals—you become like-minded. As you read God's Word together, you learn God's ways of handling problems and roadblocks that come your way. And you develop a more keen sense of His will for your marriage and life.

When you begin to realize how serious God is about marriage and how He desires to bless it—I think it further cements your hearts so you can go the distance. Even during hard times you'll know He goes before you.

Lastly, spiritual intimacy is a great way to express love. When I know that Tim is seeking God's face and is dedicated to loving me, even concerned about my spiritual growth and ours together, that provides safety and to me is the deepest expression of his love. It challenges me to love in the same way.

## FINAL THOUGHTS:

In *The Soul Care Bible*, Larry Crabb wrote an article about knowing God in which he states:

God invites us . . . to find Him, and He lets us know that in the process of finding Him, we will also find ourselves. Until we are moved to know Him with a passion that we feel nowhere else, we will not use the struggles of life as an impetus to know God. Until our passion for finding God is deeper than any other passion, we will arrange our lives according to our taste, not God's. God knows everything about us, everything about you, everything about your spouse. He is aware of our struggles that we have, and He longs for us to know Him through His Son, Jesus Christ. He is the answer to our problems. To believe in Christ is faith. To wait for Him is hope. To serve Him is love. That is what it means to find God. It is a passion to trust a sovereign Savior who will reveal the Father in response to faith in Him.

My prayer for you is that God will put the desire, the yearning within you to pursue spiritual intimacy like you've never pursued it before. Hopefully, as a woman and as a couple, you will be able to say with the apostle Paul, "I have fought the good fight, I have finished the race, I have kept the faith" (2 Timothy 4:7). May God richly bless you in your faith journey.

## ABOUT THE AUTHOR

Julie Clinton is the director and host of the Extraordinary Women video series and coauthor of *The Marriage You've Always Wanted*. She is the former director of the Liberty Godparent Home and elementary school at Lynchburg Christian Academy. She holds a B.S. degree from Liberty University, an M.A. from Lynchburg College, and an M.B.A. from Liberty University.

## VERSES THAT INSPIRE

Come near to God and he will come near to you. (James 4:8)

[God is] not far from each one of us. (Acts 17:27)

Be joyful in hope, patient in suffering, faithful in prayer. (Romans 12:12)

By wisdom a house is built,

    and through understanding it is established;

through knowledge its rooms are filled

    with rare and beautiful treasures.

    (Proverbs 24:3–4)

# Sexual Fulfillment in Marriage

JOYCE PENNER

*He is my beloved and I am His. His banner over me is love.*
*His presence sustains and refreshes me. I am lovesick.*
*His left hand is under my head, and his right hand embraces me.*
*He is all I've ever dreamt of and more.*
—ADAPTED FROM SONG OF SOLOMON

When I was a young girl, I always had an eagerness to know God and understand His Word and His will for my life. After I married, I was particularly curious about God's intentions for me in my sexual relationship with my husband.

Since I was raised in a Mennonite home and community where sexuality just wasn't discussed, I was uncertan about the pleasure we were enjoying with each other. So my husband and I searched the Scriptures to try to understand what the Bible teaches about sex. It proved to be a wonderful experience during that first year of our marriage. We discovered that God indeed affirms us as sexual persons and intends for us to delight in each other sexually in marriage.

It was twelve years later that we began writing and teaching about sexuality from a Christian perspective. Now after more than twenty-five years of counseling others, we have received hundreds of questions from couples seeking insight into God's design for a sexual relationship in marriage—how it works, concerns they have, and help they need. Let me share two e-mails I recently received. One woman writes, "After our daughter was born a year ago, I wasn't interested in sex, but it didn't bother me. I was sure that with time, things would get better. Now twelve months have gone by and, if anything, it's gotten worse. Before the birth of our child, my husband and I were sexually active. Can you tell me how to increase my desire for sex? I love my husband very much and hate that we are experiencing these problems." And an older woman wrote, "I simply can't remember a time when I experienced a physical desire for sexual relationships. This is haunting me forever. I decided years ago just to let it go, that I was not normal, and I never would be. Is it too late for me?"

The apostle Paul was faced with similar questions when believers asked him, "Is it a good thing to have sexual relations?" "Certainly," he answers, "but only within a certain context. It's good for a man to have a wife and for a woman to have a husband. Sexual drives are strong, but marriage is strong enough to contain them and provide for a balanced and fulfilling life in a world of sexual disorder.

The apostle Paul wasn't only addressing men in this text. He assumes sexual drives are strong for both men and women. Yet there are many women who do not feel sexual desire. Many other women are not fulfilling their sexual desires, nor are they experiencing a satisfactory sexual relationship with their husband. The question we need to ask is, How can women embrace their God-given sexuality? For insight, let's look at the Song of Solomon, where Solomon's wife explicitly talks about her desire for her husband.

Solomon affirms and connects with his wife. In response to his adoration of her, his wife invites amorous intimate activity: "May he kiss me with the kisses of his mouth! For your love is better than wine. . . . On my bed night after night I sought him Whom my soul loves. . . . Come, my beloved, let us go into the country, let us spend the night in the villages, let us rise early and go to the vineyards, let us see whether the vine has budded and its blossoms have opened and whether the pomegranates have bloomed. There I will give you my love" (Song of Solomon 1:2; 3:1; 7:11–12 NASB). This speaks of the pleasure we can derive as godly, sexual women—not out of a sense of duty, but because we feel loved and desired for who we are.

Through our experience of teaching a biblical perspective of sexuality, as well as maintaining a private practice as sexual therapists, my husband and I are convinced that God's intention for us is sexual contentment and containment in singleness, and sexual fulfillment and enjoyment in marriage. My passion is to help you discover who you are as a sexual person and to find and embrace the vitality sex brings to all aspects of life.

Even though this chapter is about you as a woman embracing your sexuality, our book *Men and Sex* will help your husband understand his part in making your role possible by loving you as Christ loves the church. Ephesians 5:25–28 teaches God's expectation for married men in their sexual relationship with their wife. The apostle Paul instructs husbands to go all out in their love for their wives exactly as Christ did for the church—a love marked by giving, not getting. And how did Christ love the church? Look at Philippians 2:5–8: He gave up His rights. And likewise, men sometimes have to give up their sexual rights. It says, "Think of yourselves the way Christ thought of Himself. When the time came, He set aside His privileges. He became like us so that He would know us." The husband's role is to understand exactly where his wife is emotionally and spiritually before proceeding to the sexual. Christ loved us before we responded to Him. The wife must experience her husband's unconditional love and attention in order to give herself freely to him.

Whether we're considering the husband's role or the wife's role, as a couple the basic biblical teaching for sex in marriage is the concept of mutuality. Simply stated, this concept is that both individuals come together in order to share themselves freely with each other, enjoying the pleasure of each other's bodies—but never at the expense of the other. When this occurs as God intended, there inevitably is mutuality. 1 Corinthians 7 tells us that the marriage bed is a place of mutuality—the husband seeking to satisfy his wife and the wife seeking to satisfy her husband. When we choose to commit ourselves to another in marriage, we have decided to give ourselves to our spouse, both in bed and out. Marriage is not the place to stand up for our rights.

## THE WOMAN'S ROLE FOR SEX IN MARRIAGE

### Enjoy Sex

The woman's role for sex in marriage is to know herself sexually and to share herself with her husband. In order to do this, she must be able to enjoy sex, listen to her body, lead by invitation, and heal from past or present hurts.

What are some of the ways we can enhance our ability to enjoy sex?

1. *Discard unrealistic expectations.* Sex is not going to be what you see in the media or read in romance novels. Instead, look to real people in your life who will share what has brought them fulfillment. Become knowledgeable about how the body and how you work sexually.

2. *Learn to receive compliments, bodily pleasure, and sexual stimulation.* The capacity in which each of you can do this depends on how you feel about yourself. Women who have a poor self-image have difficulty accepting pleasure in general, and consequently they have a harder time enjoying sex.

3. *Accept your body.* If you don't, it's very difficult for you to share your body with your husband. To increase your comfort with your appearance, eliminate unrealistic ideals and focus on what would help you feel good about your body. There's nothing wrong with setting a standard for yourself. It may require a variety of disciplines, like exercising, watching what you eat, going for occasional pedicures, or having your hair professionally maintained. The way in which you care for yourself has a great impact on how you feel about yourself.

4. *Allow intimacy with your husband.* Intimacy suggests

vulnerability. To be loved for who you are requires total openness with your husband, particularly when you come together sexually. Some women have difficulty with this type of emotional and physical closeness because they fear they will lose their sense of individuality. A fear of intimacy is usually related to a fear of abandonment. Maybe you struggle with such issues from your childhood, when circumstances prevented your parents from being there when you needed them. Intimacy is an attachment, a connection with another person. It's not based on infatuation or attraction. Intimacy becomes more apparent when the newness of a relationship evolves into a deep attachment that will carry you through the life of your marriage.

5. *Enjoy newness.* A certain sense of freedom is also important for you to take pleasure in a sexual relationship. Be flexible, be willing to experiment, and try new things. Newness creates excitement, and flexibility fosters freedom. Give yourself permission to experiment in touching your mate, as well as in allowing him to explore your body.

6. *Affirm your sexuality.* You are a sexual being. You were designed this way by God. Within five to ten minutes after

birth, a little boy has his first sexual response in terms of arousal. Baby girls lubricate vaginally within twenty-four hours after birth. And those responses continue automatically and involuntarily throughout life. Just as your body digests food, your heart beats, and your lungs breathe, your sexuality is automatic. Your body was created to both receive and transmit sexual stimulation. If women think of themselves as the receptacles of their husband's sexual aggression, they are rejecting God's intention for them. You were made to both receive and to transmit sexual pleasure.

> *Intimacy becomes more apparent when the newness of a relationship evolves into a deep attachment that will carry you through the life of your marriage.*

By the way, did you know that women who enjoy sex can also say *no?* We can't freely say yes to sex unless we can also say no. In that way, our sexual relationship is similar to our relationship with God. Christ sacrificed Himself for us and asked only that we accept Him as our Lord and Savior. But He never forces Himself on us. We have the freedom of choice. And that has to be true in the sexual relationship between you and your husband. To freely give yourself sexually, you must be free to make a choice.

7. *Learn to let go.* Women who enjoy sex learn to become caught up in the moment, to experience the freedom of being out of control, and to delight in the ecstasy of an orgasm. In order to do this, you may need help to release anything in your relationship with your husband that might hinder intimacy, such as unresolved issues or unforgiveness. If you take personal issues against your spouse to bed with you, the ability to let go and enjoy sex are hindered by your negative thoughts and feelings.

So to enjoy sex and experience a passionate marriage, a woman needs need to believe she is worthy of her husband's attention and that she has the right to be intensely sexual. She has to be able to affirm her sexuality, her husband's sexuality, her husband's delight in her sexuality, and her enjoyment of his sexuality. Sex has to be as good for her as it is for him, if it's going to be fulfilling for the lifetime of a marriage. The best gift a woman can give herself and her husband is a deep and real joy in their sexual times together.

## Listen to Your Body

To fulfill your role for sex in marriage, you need to not only enjoy sex, but also learn to listen to your body. Good sex doesn't just happen, but we can make it happen by listening to our bodies. Pay attention to your body during your daily activities. Take note of momentary desires that come and go throughout the day. Listen during sex, when you and your husband are pleasuring each other. What feels good? What kind of touch do you like? How do you like to be kissed? Take it in and absorb it. Enjoy those sensations of being touched. And listen to what your body is saying. Both partners win when the woman listens to her body and seeks what she needs, while the man listens and responds to her desires.

## Lead by Invitation

Once you've learned to listen to your body and enjoy sex, you will be able to lead by invitation. The model from the Song of Solomon, as well as other instruction throughout Scripture, demonstrates that the husband adores while his wife invites. This scenario works because a woman's expression of her sexuality usually appeals to a man, whereas a man's expression of connection and affirmation usually appeals to a woman.

For you to lead with your sexuality, you have to know your body and share your awareness with your husband. With his help you can discover what brings you pleasure. You have to attend to and take responsibility for the hormonal fluctuations that affect you during the month and throughout the different stages of life. For example, early marriage is different than five years down the road with kids. Pregnancy is a change that affects your hormones. As you move into menopause, your body changes again. Being attentive to what your body needs today and to its changes is key to being able to lead with your sexuality and communicate what brings you pleasure.

The belief that, "If he loved me, he would really know," doesn't work. It's like an itch on our back. If we ask him to scratch it for us, we have to explain where it is or he won't know. That's also true about our body awareness and sexual desires. Sex will never be great if you expect him to automatically know how, where, and when you want to be touched.

To lead, you must also know and communicate your

conditions for good sex. What makes sex good for you? Do you need to be rested? Do you need to feel a special connection between the two of you? What moments have brought you the most joy? What were the conditions that contributed to the uniqueness of those experiences? Communicating those conditions will not only make sex better for you, but also for your husband. Your husband can't know and meet your complex and diverse sexual needs unless you guide him.

The truth is that sexually we are more complex than men—in both our sexual organs and our bodily responses. Fluctuations occur due to our hormonal changes. Our bodily responses are physically more complex, and sexually we function on two tracks: the emotional and the physical. These two must be in sync in order for us to open ourselves sexually. The good news in all of this is that our complex, ever-changing femininity combined with our husband's predictability can be used to keep sex alive in marriage over a lifetime.

## Heal from Past or Present Hurts

However, to enjoy sex, listen to your body, and lead by invitation, you must first heal from past or present abuse. If you were sexually or physically abused as a child, experienced trauma as an adolescent or young adult, were raised in an alcoholic home, or are in an abusive relationship now, it is imperative that you take the time to heal those wounds. You may need a Christian counselor, a recovery group, a mentor, or a good friend who will come alongside you and walk you through those resurfaced hurts, in order to move beyond them. The reality is, healing will take time and work.

## WHEN SEX ISN'T WORKING

### He Wants Sex, You Don't—Now What?

What do you do if he wants sex but you don't? If you are like the women who e-mail us who aren't interested in sex, ask yourself a few questions.

1) *Is all your energy being consumed elsewhere?* Your sexual energy and your drive to accomplish things come from the same source. If you're using it up on your kids, a job, or the pressures of life, you many not have anything left for your sexual relationship.

Women with young children are exhausted when they

fall into bed at night. You and your husband should sit down and talk about this. Taking a daily nap became routine for me after our first daughter was born and has been an important part of my life every since. I set a timer for thirty minutes, even though I often wake up before then, but taking that break is so important to revitalize me. And it's not selfish to take this time for yourself. Consider it an investment in your marriage. Another way to regain energy may be to have somebody come to your home and take care of the kids for a little while each day. Maybe a neighbor girl on the street can play with your children while you take a break. Soak in a tub with a good book, go for a walk, get your hair done, or go to the library, but do something to refresh your energy.

2) *Are you having sex by demand?* Women who were eager for sex when they first married and over time find themselves pressured more and more by their husbands for sex will lose interest quickly. His demands stifle her desire. If your husband's mood or his sense of worth depends on your interest in him sexually, it will cause havoc in the relationship. In time, your sexual desire will decrease until there's nothing left

but bitterness and resentment. You will feel inadequate because what you give is never enough. And it never will be enough because sex isn't what it's about. Sex is not about keeping your husband happy. Sex is about sharing yourself openly and freely and giving yourself to one another in order to experience a mutual delight in being together. Sexual force-feeding in marriage leads to sexual anorexia.

3) *Are your hormones out of balance?* If you are reaching menopause, don't be surprised if your sex drive has diminished. However, even young women may lack desire because of hormonal imbalance. When testosterone levels dip, so does your sexual desire. All the effort in the world won't work if your hormones are out of balance. The best thing you can do is go to your doctor and ask for a complete hormone panel, including a free, or bioavailable, testosterone level.

All women have three hormones: estrogen, progesterone, and testosterone. A hormone test will reveal any deficiencies in our hormone levels. I think of estrogen as the "happy hormone." It keeps us content and alive with a sense of well-being. Progesterone is our "relaxation hormone," and testosterone is our "drive hormone." We often think of testosterone as the male hormone, but women need it too. If your free (or bioavailable) testosterone is low, you won't have energy and may even struggle with depression. This can be corrected by using a testosterone cream. Your physician will need to assist you in these decisions.

4) *Are you waiting to be zapped?* Are you looking for the feelings of newness and attraction rather than deep, caring attachment? Stop and consider what it was that attracted you to your husband when you first met. Reflect on those times that brought you together. Initial attraction has to shift into long-term attachment or intimacy. The shift takes place anywhere from six months to thirty months after you start a sexual relationship or get married. If you don't make that shift, you may feel like you no longer love him or you're no longer attracted to him. When you confuse the change in feeling with love, you may experience hopelessness. Instead, get help in learning to discover a new type of passion based on long-term, intimate connection.

Actually, you don't have to experience desire in order to initiate sex. In fact, you can counter sexual disinterest by making the conscious choice to have sex. It's fine to make love with your husband when he wants to, as long as you're not against it. When you are unwilling, those are times to just enjoy being touched and being close without any need to go for sexual arousal or release.

## You Want It and He Doesn't

Contrary to common belief, men are not always "in the mood" for sex. Women and men tend to think that all men want sex all the time. If your husband doesn't want sex, you may feel badly about yourself and worry that you're not attractive to him. Share those feelings with him, but don't blame or nag him. Nagging will never result in more sex. Rather, reach out to touch him. Rub his shoulders, arms, and legs. Enjoy the pleasure of his body without any pressure for him to respond. Let your husband know when you want to have sex. Sometimes women expect only the man to initiate sex. But that's kind of a game we play. If you're the interested party, take responsibility to pursue it. But initiate it physically rather than verbally, unless that doesn't work in your situation.

## Your Past Is in Control

When your past affects your present sexual relationship, it

can cause devastation. And when your past controls you, it can manifest itself in different ways. If you were raised in an alcoholic home, you may feel confused about sex. Because your parents weren't in control, you internalized the need for control. And now, in a sexual encounter, when you feel out of control you get very uncomfortable. You must recognize your need for control and make it work for you rather than against you. Plan your sexual times. Take charge in a positive way.

Women who were sexually abused as children might experience a flashback during a moment of adult lovemaking that's similar to their childhood trauma. It can be nothing more than a simple touch or a word that snaps you back to that horrifying experience. There are several ways to counteract this. First, talk about it outside of the bedroom, and arrange to signal your husband to let him know when you are having an uncomfortable reaction. Men who are married to women who have been sexually abused need to have God-given patience and understanding, as well as a willingness to help their wife work through these difficulties. When you experience flashbacks, try to stay connected with your husband. Keep eye contact with him and remind yourself that he is your trusted mate and not the abuser. It may help you to talk to him throughout the lovemaking in order to keep yourself connected to the present.

If a woman was aroused as a child through pictures or fantasy, she may have difficulty experiencing an orgasm without them. Usually this connection begins when a young girl finds her dad's stash of pornography or reads and responds to a romance novel with explicit sexual details. She becomes hooked on that fantasy or picture and can't sexually respond without visualizing it. We encourage women in this situation to stay actively engaged and talk out a new fantasy with their husband that will replace those old fantasies. Exchange your fantasy for something good, even if it's a little bit titillating or exciting or different than your ordinary sexual encounters. For example, imagine you and your husband on a deserted island, or on an exotic adventure that doesn't connect with those old images that cause you guilt or conflict.

Of course, if you had prior sexual partners in your life, you may find it difficult not to compare them with your husband. Again, we recommend that you "stay in the moment" with your mate.

## Anger, Shame, or Guilt Have Invaded the Bedroom

Unresolved anger is often the by-product of a relationship that is void of affection outside the marital bed, with aggressive sexual advances. But a woman's anger must be dealt with before she can find satisfying intimacy with her husband.

## Sex Is Painful

There are some women who avoid sex because it's physically painful for them. Since sex is designed for pleasure, painful sex should not be allowed to continue. Talk to your physician and try to find someone who specializes in dyspaeunia, or painful intercourse. It will help if you can identify exactly where it hurts and what triggers the pain during lovemaking. For example, if muscle tightness is a problem, you will need to use something, like a series of dilators, to stretch that muscle. You may need to do muscle exercises that control the opening of your vagina. If you learn how to tighten and relax those muscles, you can gain control. Relaxation techniques may help. Physical therapy may ultimately be necessary if you can't learn to relax the muscles on your own.

If you experience a stinging sensation during sex, changing your diet can make a difference. Avoid sugar, caffeine, and citrus fruits. Identify and avoid any foods that you're allergic to. Make sure your body is in a healthy balance. A vitamin-mineral supplement often helps.

If you experience deep, stabbing pain, try changing positions during intercourse. What sometimes occurs during sex is that the penis thrusts against the cervix, or the opening of the uterus. Changing the angle of entry may help.

If you experience vaginal dryness or irritation, hormonal replacement therapy is the most helpful solution. There are also natural ways to incease lubrication. There's a tablet that can be inserted in the vagina called Vagifem. Ask your doctor to prescribe it. It's inserted once a day for two weeks, then one tablet, twice a week. It often clears up any vaginal irritation and dryness.

## You Can't Let Go

Perhaps you enjoyed sex a great deal in the early part of your marriage, but you were unable to experience an orgasm. Over time, your interest in sex declined. When a woman can't climax because she gets aroused, comes close to an orgasm, but then plateaus out, eventually her sexual desire becomes extinguished. To help your body let go, you can practice what we call "sexual triggers," such as making noises, moving, throwing your head back, pointing your toes, or whatever. If you exaggerate those actions, you can trigger an orgasm.

Additionally, avoid watching yourself during intercourse. Sex is not a spectator sport. Abandon yourself and enter into the moment rather than wait for your response. Watching hinders the natural response.

## Talking Hasn't Helped

If sex isn't working in your marriage and you haven't been able to talk about it as a couple, you may need to get help. Communicating is vital to keeping love, passion, and intimacy alive in your sex life. Yet many couples do not know how to talk or share openly about their sex lives. Or maybe they've experienced so much conflict whenever they try, so they have given up. Try to talk with one another without evaluating and with as much expression of care and affirmation as you can. Use "I" statements to express how you feel. And ultimately, if you can't work it out on your own, seek professional help. Be sure to keep searching until you discover the sexual pleasure you so desire and God wants for you.

## HOW TO MAKE SEX BETTER

### A Formula for Intimacy

Great sex doesn't just happen. But when we are intentional about our sexual relationship, sex can be fantastic. Protect your marriage. Don't let children, work, friends, or church get in the way. You have to carve out time for one another. In addition, you must guard your heart, aware that all of us are vulnerable to outside temptations. Make sure that all of your sexual thoughts and interests stay focused on your spouse. If anything makes you feel aroused, bring your spouse's face into that picture and turn those feelings toward him and act on those feelings with him. Don't pursue those fantasies with anyone else.

To work at sex and to protect your marriage, you have to deliberately set aside time to be intimate. Schedule rather than wait for spontaneity. A lot of people say, "Schedule sex? Doesn't that take the romance out of it?" Think of dating. Remember how you scheduled time to be together? Those were some of your best times of connecting and learning about each other. Likewise, when you anticipate sex because you're planning for it, your lovemaking will have much better quality and will tend to occur more often.

The formula for intimacy that we recommend is:

> 15 minutes per day
>
> 1 evening per week
>
> ½ or 1 day per month
>
> 1 weekend per season

We suggest that couples allow fifteen minutes a day just for the two of them, to focus on one another. During this time, don't talk about who's picking up the kids or the dry cleaning or who's doing the dishes that night. It's a time to talk about you and your husband and how you feel and how he feels. You may think fifteen minutes isn't enough, but fifteen minutes is a whole lot better than nothing. After taking some time to talk, share something spiritually—a Bible verse or a prayer. Then end with thirty seconds or a couple of minutes of passionate kissing. On your designated evening a week, or "date night," you might go out together or just take time to enjoy one another's conversation and have some fun at home. The monthly or seasonal times may be more difficult to arrange, but when you can arrange them, you will cherish those times. I am convinced that if every couple practiced this formula for intimacy, the divorce rate would drop significantly and there would be much higher sexual satisfaction in marriage.

## Make Sex Work for You

It goes without saying that men and women are different. For this reason, as husbands and wives, we need to make our sexual differences work for us. The husband needs to spend time cherishing his wife. As she feels loved, she will open sexually and invite him. Both partners will be happy. But make sure sex doesn't always mean sex. Sometimes you need to just have fun and play together. Lighten up. Maintain a childlike spirit. Roll, giggle, be silly, and exaggerate.

Recall how you used to have fun together. Relive some of those old experiences. Flirt with your husband, romance him the way you once did, and daydream about him. Focus on your similarities rather than your differences, and always try to make sure that you counter every negative interaction with five positives.

Finally, kiss one another passionately. We are convinced that passionate kissing is a true barometer of a sexual relationship. Couples who no longer kiss long and deep are no longer having fulfilling sexual lives. You may wonder, *How do we start?* It is natural to feel awkward when you haven't been kissing for a long time. We recommend that you start very deliberately. Consider this kissing exercise that we recommend to couples: Take turns and teach each other how to use your mouth and tongue and lips with each other. In other words, you kiss him and he is the recipient. You're teaching him how you like to kiss, and he's following your lead. Then he shows you how he likes to be kissed. It's fun! Even if kissing is going well in your relationship, try it. It gives you a chance to talk about kissing, which helps you explore ways to enjoy each other. Then make kissing a part

of your life; don't go to bed until you have kissed passionately.

## ABOUT THE AUTHOR

Joyce Penner is a columnist for *Marriage Partnership.* As a
clinical nurse specializing in psychosomatic disorders, she has
practiced as a sexual, marital, and premarital therapist for
twenty-five years. She is Associate Pastor of Congregational
Life at Lake Avenue Church in Pasadena, California, as well
as the author or co-author of nine books and a contributing
editor for *Marriage & Family: A Christian Journal.* She is also
a veteran in the field as a conference speaker and media personality.

## VERSES THAT INSPIRE

> The husband should fulfill his marital duty to his
> wife, and likewise the wife to her husband. The

wife's body does not belong to her alone but also to her husband. In the same way, the husband's body does not belong to him alone but also to his wife. Do not deprive each other except by mutual consent and for a time, so that you may devote yourselves to prayer. (1 Corinthians 7:3–5)

Marriage should be honored by all, and the marriage bed kept pure, for God will judge the adulterer and all the sexually immoral. (Hebrews 13:4)

May you rejoice in the wife of your youth. . . . May her breasts satisfy you always. May you ever be captivated by her love. (Proverbs 5:18–19)

And [God] said, "For this reason a man will leave his father and mother and be united to his wife, and the two will become one flesh . . ." So they are no longer two, but one. Therefore what God has joined together, let man not separate.
(Matthew 19:5–6)

Let him kiss me with the kisses of his mouth—

    for your love is more delightful than wine.

Pleasing is the fragrance of your perfumes,

    your name is like perfume poured out.

    No wonder the maidens love you!

Take me away with you—let us hurry!

    Let the king bring me into his chambers.

(Song of Solomon 1:2–4)

# Making Your Marriage a Great Marriage

BARBARA ROSBERG

*[Be] strengthened with all power according to his glorious*
*might so that you may have great endurance and patience.*
—COLOSSIANS 1:11

Recently I sat down for coffee with a very good friend who
told me what was on her mind. "Barb," she said, "my husband and I are experiencing a time in our lives and I'm hurting because we're not connecting. We're going through some
tough times, but to be perfectly honest, I feel kind of guilty
even mentioning this to you."

"What you're going through is just a good case of the 'normal' drifting apart that can occur in marriage," I explained. "Tell me, what's at the bottom of it?"

For this couple, the conflict centered on his preoccupation with his career. They had both initially been excited about his career move, but it eventually became a mistress, stealing away her husband's attention. There's an old saying: "The mistress gets the flowers." In this case, the mistress was his job, as well as some volunteer work he had committed to. Something was distracting her husband from being attentive to his wife's heart; her needs were not being met by the man God had given her. There was clearly a breakdown in their communication and she was really becoming discouraged. They just didn't have any talk time. The romance is really gone from a marriage when a couple no longer talks about anything other than family logistics.

She looked at me and asked, "What do we do?"

I sat back, relieved. Every married couple goes through periods of disconnecting with one another. And every couple needs more time together to talk. Men and women are very different, but we're all made in the image of God. Many of us begin our marriages thinking, *I'm going to change my mate.* And that's the worst thing we can do.

Let me share my story. In our early years as a married couple, Gary was working on his doctorate, going to graduate school and working full time. We had two little girls and I was home with those babies. And this was the crux of the problem: I looked to Gary to meet my emotional needs, but he was distracted, actually driven by his "mistress"—school and work. The girls and I saw very little of him.

The funny thing is, when he started the graduate program, we were both excited about it. It takes two to have a career and to muddle through schooling. But through years of stress and endless demands—many days Gary left before 7:00 in the morning and didn't get home until 10:30 at night—I ended up feeling isolated and discouraged and I pulled away from Gary, my best friend. This discord between us hurt my heart. I would plead with him; I'd tell him I needed more time with him as my husband, that the girls needed their dad. But yet, as a man, he longed to climb the career ladder. So I think he stopped listening when I talked with him. It must have sounded like nagging. I'd pray and try to figure out solutions. I'd tell him, "You know, maybe you could spend a little less time at the library and more time with your family." But when he didn't change, over time I began to disconnect and slowly I quit talking to him. I'd think to myself, *Why try?* And I'm sure my husband thought, *Whew, she's moved beyond that.* But over time this tension between us hardened my heart toward Gary. Gary no longer felt like a safe harbor for me. I needed to talk, and I needed emotional connection with him. You see, Gary had been my best friend, but I felt hurt and discouraged by the drifing apart in our relationship. And this is why I understood perfectly when my friend came to me for help with a similar situation in her marriage.

If you've learned anything, I hope it's this: When you get discouraged in your marriage, you need to talk to a godly woman who's a little bit older, a little bit wiser, and a little bit farther down the road who can give you some encouragement to stay the course and hang in there. There are seasons when marriages undergo turmoil, where husbands and wives feel emotionally distant. It's during those trials that we come to the end of ourselves and turn to our relationship with God to learn what we truly need to experience a great marriage.

Looking back on those early years of our marriage, Gary and I realize they were some of the hardest days we've ever endured. But in the long run, we learned to communicate at a level like no other couple I know. Finally we figured out how to get back in touch with one another even though Gary was so busy. When he came home at 10:30 at night, we sat down and talked from the heart from 10:30 until 11:30. We talked about what I had endured during the day and what he had grappled with. But we also discussed what we needed from each other.

> *Eventually we came to see that our hope was in Christ, not in each other.*

Eventually we came to see that our hope was in Christ, not in each other. It's an amazing thing. With all my talking and pleading, and then my heart shutting down for a period of time in our marriage, it was amazing to see how God answered my prayers once I relied upon Him.

One day our five-year-old daughter, Sarah, brought Gary a piece of paper with a drawing on it.

"Daddy, Daddy, do you want to see my picture of the family?" she asked him.

"Not right now, Sarah. I've got to study," he answered. But since he was working on his doctorate in counseling, he knew right away he had said the wrong thing. He called her back. She ran to him and climbed up on his lap. The picture showed Mommy and Katie, our Irish setter, and Missy, her little sister, who occupied a large part of the page, and then Sarah. But there was no Daddy in the picture.

"Daddy, do you like my picture?" she asked.

"Yes, Sarah. But where's Daddy?"

"Daddy, you're at the library studying," she answered as she jumped down and ran off. Well, the most amazing thing happened in my husband's heart as he stared at that picture. He was devastated. For the first time, in spite of months of my pleading, it all finally made sense through a simple drawing from a five-year-old girl.

But things didn't change overnight. Several months later, Gary and I were lying in bed. In the middle of the night he turned to me and said, "Barb, are you awake?"

"Yes."

"I have a question for you. Can I come home?"

"Gary, I love you. Your daughters love you. But nobody knows you," I replied. In that moment I also realized how much he was suffering and how isolated he felt from his family. This was exactly what I'd been praying for—that Gary would recognize how much he was needed—but it had to be in God's timing, not mine.

## THE FIVE "LOVE NEEDS"

From this difficult period in our marriage Gary and I recognized that every man and woman has basic, God-given needs that must be met by their mate. Once we identified these needs, we decided to write about them. We asked 1,400 people across America, "What are the top five love needs that must be met by your mate in order for you to have a great marriage?" Many times people just can't answer that question because they don't even know what their top five love needs are. But women across America told us that their husbands needed unconditional love, emotional intimacy, spiritual intimacy with their wife, encouragement, and better friendships.

1. *Unconditional Love.* Interestingly enough, the number one love need for women is unconditional love—the same need as for their husband. But unconditional love is not humanly possible. Unconditional love only comes from one source—Jesus Christ. We can only acquire unconditional love from a relationship with Him. If you've surrendered your life to the Lord, you understand that His love is the kind of love that loves us even when we hit our weakest point, even when we've disappointed ourselves and those we love, and even when we've failed miserably.

It was in those rough early years of our marriage that Gary and I discovered the true source of unconditional love. Women simply cannot be loved by their husbands in this way. I found this love in my relationship with the Lord when I was hurting the most; and Gary found it when he was suffering the most. When we finally realize who Christ is in our life and we seek to have our emptiness filled by Him and Him alone, we are able to love others much more fully.

To be loved unconditionally, women need to be loved at their greatest point of pain. Of course, pain varies from woman to woman. If you've suffered any kind of loss (maybe through death or divorce, or even being abandoned by your father when you were young), you are really going to need the true, unconditional love of the Father lived out through your husband to help you get through this.

So how can a husband meet his wife's need for unconditional love? We need the assurance that we are loved just as we are and that our husbands will stick by us no matter what. We also need our husbands to remind us that God loves us and to seek comfort in His love. After all, our true source of fulfillment comes from an audience of One—Jesus Christ. Women are usually connected to their husbands, their children, their careers, and the people in their lives, and as a result, they strive to be pleasers rather than to be pleasing. But the bottom line is, you can't please everybody. When your life ends, there will be an audience of One—Jesus Christ, before whom we will lay our lives. Live your life for an audience of One and you'll be sure to please God.

Our husbands also need to realize that loving us unconditionally is highlighted by their response to our failures or disappointments. Those responses are critical. The first thing he says after we've shared a particularly trying situation will determine whether we fold or whether we rise above the circumstances. So when we've failed, when we're discouraged, words like, "I will always be here for you" or, "You never have to perform or earn my love. I love you no matter what," can inspire us not to give up.

A few years ago I noticed real growth in our marriage. I became aware of it at the first Promise Keepers event at which Gary was speaking. I joined him on that trip in order to pray and support him. Little did I know what would soon unfold. At the very end of Gary's talk, in front of 60,000 men, he said, "And now I'm going to ask my wife Barb to come up. She didn't know I was going to do this."

I couldn't believe he was doing this. My heart was beating like no other time in my life. So I went up on the platform but I didn't dare look out at those 60,000 people or I was sure I'd die from shock. As I sat down in the chair he offered me, I could barely comprehend his words. Suddenly he held a Bible above me, then read from the Gospel of John. I heard him say, "'No,' said Peter, 'you shall never wash my feet'" (John 13:8). And I thought to myself, *You're not going to wash my feet. Nobody's ever washed my feet.* But that's exactly what he did. He bent down and in front of all those men he removed my shoes and washed my feet with his handkerchief. As he did so, he cried and asked me to forgive him, so that he could love me more like Christ loves him. In that moment, I realized that my husband really wanted to love me like Christ loves me. I can make mistakes, I can challenge him, and I can even drive him crazy at times, but his love for me will not fade. And in front of 60,000 people, my husband changed my life. He demonstrated to me, beyond all reason, the power of being loved—loved like Christ loves each one of us.

2. *Emotional Intimacy.* The second love need women have is emotional intimacy with their husbands. Once love is irrevocably established, how can a couple achieve deeper intimacy in their marriage? Not surprisingly, the men and women who were surveycd responded this way about intimacy: Men spelled it S-E-X and women spelled it T-A-L-K. If for any reason they're neglected, women will withdraw from their mates. Perhaps it's been an especially long time since there was a chance to talk. Tensions build and we tend to stifle

our feelings when the pace of life becomes hectic. If this continues, a husband and wife can end up as two strangers living under the same roof, sharing the same bed, but with very little intimacy taking place. You know what else happens? To your husband, it appears you are rejecting his advances when he initiates lovemaking. Problem is, you're not rejecting him; you just can't respond physically when you feel so emotionally distant. Conflicts need to be resolved before we allow ourselves to participate in sex.

And if your emotional needs are not met, you become vulnerable. If it's not taken care of one way, something or someone else will fill the void. Maybe you'll fill the void through a career, or maybe you'll spend more time on your children or more time with your friends. But here's the bottom line: If your husband is not meeting your need for emotional intimacy, you run the risk of becoming involved with another man. Many times your need for emotional intimacy can lead you down a road of destruction that is so subtle you don't even realize where you're headed. If your husband has wounded you in some way, if you're in conflict with him, if you're not committed to the relationship, if your heart has shut down and you quit trying, then you're extremely vulnerable to another man's attention or affection.

In this frame of mind, it's easy to look at someone else's husband and think he's the ideal man. We begin to compare other men to our husband, magnifying his flaws and minimizing our commitment. This leads to developing a relationship with other men we know, like our boss, a neighbor, or even our best friend's husband. We begin to sense a bond with this other man. When we begin to think in terms of meeting him or being with him, we are headed for disaster. If you are contemplating a future with a man other than your mate, or if you think you have a chance with another woman's husband, you are living in a fantasy. If you really want a godly marriage and a great relationship with your spouse, you have to challenge these thoughts and fantasies. If there are areas of conflict with your husband, you need to address them and work through them together.

Women are emotionally wired. As a result, we need to guard our heart. Don't become captive to your emotions. It's critical that every woman know that the very man they're searching for is actually the one they're married to. Perhaps you've become emotionally blinded and don't see all that he is because he's hurt you emotionally. If I'm describing you or someone you know, there are some steps to take, with God's help, to resolve this.

First of all, you need to admit that these kinds of thoughts open the door to the destruction of your marriage, as well as your family. The second thing you need to do is bring it before the Lord and confess it. Deal with those issues in your heart that need to be forgiven. Then take action to resist these kinds of thoughts through the power of God's Spirit. Take them to the cross for clarity and peace of mind. Distance yourself from the man who is distracting you from your marriage. If it's your boss, quit your job. If it's a friend of the family, quit getting together as couples. Whatever you do, run. Run into the arms of God and then run into the arms of your husband. Step a little bit closer to your husband—go to him and reaffirm your love and your commitment to him. Confess to him the issues that have prompted you to guard your heart and eventually become hardened toward him. Tell him there are issues you must work on as a couple and that you need him and love him. The purpose in this confession is that it will open up the door to your heart for your husband, which will allow him to connect with you emotionally.

There is nothing better than a husband meeting his wife's need for emotional intimacy. But he needs you to teach him how to do this. The first thing your husband needs to do is take the initiative to resolve conflict in your marriage. When issues come up, you need to agree to address them before you retire for the night. Don't go to bed angry. If there are issues from the past that keep coming up, or issues close to your heart, then take the initiative and visit with a godly counselor so you can move beyond these recurring problems. The first step toward establishing emotional intimacy in marriage is to have two clean hearts committed to one another.

Additionally, just like you, your husband needs to safeguard his heart against other women. When conversations with the opposite sex go from basic day-to-day to sharing more confidential issues, improper relationships can take root overnight. As an old English proverb puts it: "The eyes are the windows of the soul." And ladies, you have seen this happen right before your very eyes—a woman sending signals to a man. Every woman understands it perfectly, but sometimes our husbands don't. Warn them about those signals: too much flattery from a female colleague, or hugs, touches, or pats from a female friend. When you see these signals, gently and lovingly point them out to your mate in the privacy of your home.

3. *Spiritual Intimacy.* Women all across America tell us their third need is spiritual intimacy with their husband. Whether you're married or single, male or female, spiritual intimacy originates with our surrender to the King of kings and Lord of lords. It begins when we pursue a relationship with the Lord.

Many women long for a spiritual connection with their husband, but this takes two people invested and committed to their relationship. This means that the wife pursues her own relationship with the Lord, while her husband presses forward with his relationship. When two people join as one in this capacity, it turns a good marriage into a great marriage.

We all long for fellowship in our marriage. We yearn for our husband to be a spiritual sounding board, as well as our leader and guide. For some men, discussing spiritual matters feels intimidating. Perhaps he feels inadequate or unqualified spiritually. We need to encourage our husband to simply listen. We don't necessarily need answers; we simply need him to hear what we're thinking and to affirm those areas where he sees godly character being developed in our lives. We also need him to encourage us to use our spiritual gifts because we grow in the Lord as we utilize them. Serve in a church nursery, volunteer with Meals on Wheels, or mentor other women. Regardless of your gifts, when your husband affirms those areas you are involved in, you grow, mature, and become more of the woman Jesus designed you to be. This is one reason you need a spiritual connection with your husband.

*For some men, discussing spiritual matters feels intimidating.*

Spiritual intimacy, however, can be neglected if your husband fails to allow Jesus Christ to occupy the spiritual throne of his life. The throne room in his heart that should belong to God sometimes becomes cluttered with the cares of the world: work, managing finances, and other people, places, and things. When this happens, both of you are affected. You need a man who is discerning enough to clear out what doesn't belong there and to reserve it only for the Lord. It's very difficult to connect to a husband who isn't connected to the Lord. You also need a man who lives by example when it comes to the spiritual realm. You need to be married to a man who lives in private what he preaches in public. You need your husband to be a man of integrity.

Two people on a journey of spiritual intimacy grow together through prayer. Maybe you just need your husband to take your hand at mealtime and pray with you. Or maybe at the end of the day you might say to him, "Could we pray right before we go to sleep?" There's really nothing to bond you so securely as having your husband pray with you.

Before our daughter, Sarah, got married, I challenged our future son-in-law: "Scott, what if you prayed with Sarah every day before you got married up until the day you died?" And do you know, Scott has taken my challenge and he's prayed with Sarah every day. Sarah has told me it drives her crazy at times. You see, she likes to go to bed earlier than Scott, so he'll wake her up before he goes to sleep. He'll tap her on the shoulder and say, "Sarah, I need to pray with you. I want to take you before the Lord before we go to sleep tonight." The thing that bothers her the most is when she is angry with him. Still, he'll wake her up and say, "Sarah, let's go before the Father. Let's pray together." She tells me, "Mom, it melts me every time."

So pray with your mate. Ask your husband to take the steps toward pursuing spiritual intimacy. It will make a good marriage a great marriage.

4. *Encouragement.* The number four love need that women require is encouragement. There was a nun out of Morris, Minnesota, who told her seventh-grade class one afternoon, "Put away your homework. We're going to get out a sheet of blue-lined notebook paper and write down all the names of everybody in class." So they did. Then she told them, "Write down one way that the other kids in your class have impacted you." And they followed through. She then took all those pieces of paper, brought them home over the weekend, took out thirty pages of paper, and wrote down the names of different kids across the top. Then she compiled everything that each of the students had written about the

other children. On Monday morning she handed each student the piece of paper with positive words from their classmates. Immediately she knew it was a success as she saw that each child was excited to read what others had said about him or her.

Some twenty years later, one of those students named Mark Eckland went to fight for our country in Vietnam and died while fighting there. When his body was sent back to Morris, Minnesota, many of his classmates attended his funeral. Afterward, at the luncheon, Mark's father went up to the teacher and said, "When we were given Mark's valuables, including his wallet, I looked through it. Inside the wallet was a lined piece of yellowed notebook paper that had been taped in several places, obviously read and reread several times. All of those positive things his classmates had said about him, he carried with him in his wallet." Now, that's the power of encouragement.

When our husbands affirm us, when they remind us of how important we are to our family, when they say, "I think you're the best wife anybody can have," or, "Honey, I love growing old with you," or, "I appreciate your care and attention to our family," those words are worth taking to our grave, just like that young man named Mark Eckland did.

5. *Friendship*. The fifth love need of women is friendship. The truth is, we can't have friendship in our marriage if we don't spend time developing it. Here's an example of what friendship really feels like.

About forty minutes west of our house is a place where they filmed the movie *The Bridges of Madison County*. It's a fictional story, but one of the characters is a man named Richard. Richard did not talk to his wife. He was a hardworking man, and he loved his wife, Francesca, but he

> *The truth is, we can't have friendship in our marriage if we don't spend time developing it.*

struggled to express it. Rarely did he talk to her, touch her, spend time with her, or praise her. The story is simple. He doesn't meet her love needs. As a result, she becomes vulnerable and she falls to the attention and praise of another man. She didn't mean to have an affair, but rarely do people plan an affair. Robert Kincaid simply talked to her. He listened to her and he paid close attention. He laughed at her jokes. He picked flowers for her. He even cleaned up the dishes after a meal. He shared his world with her and asked about hers. He offered her a drink with respect and courtesy. Within a matter of days, Francesca's emotions were on fire, and she struggled with the awful battle within her. But she lost the battle because she had been deprived of the tenderness and love of her own husband and she turned to someone who could give it to her.

Now, don't we all long for our husbands to be the hero in a script like that? Many times we go into restaurants and we see couples who aren't talking because they are so disinterested in one another. They act as if they don't want to even talk to one another. We need the foundation of friendship to go the distance in a marriage. Our marriages begin in friendship, and friendship is the thread that will take us to the end.

Friendship with our husband is different than friendship with our women friends. Our husband needs to be our best friend. Women will come and go in our lives, but we need that one friendship to carry us through life. He'll be the one who sees us through all circumstances. When you have a friendship, you nurture it. You don't always say everything you think; you delight in bringing out the best in that person and you dream dreams together. We need our husband to share our dreams and ask us what they are. Let him know your heart. Dream your dreams together. Set new goals. If you have an empty nest like Gary and I do, than it's more important that you set new goals, just like you did when you were newly married. Make sure you continue to reinforce the foundation of friendship in your marriage, so you won't end up like that couple sitting across the table in the cool stage, not knowing what to say to one another. We love to be around people we like, so make sure you spend time working through issues so you can develop the friendship aspect of marriage.

Remember, you can have a good marriage, but if you want a great marriage, you really need a marriage of three: Two people to be surrendered to God, who designed marriage. We need more of God in our marriage and less of us. Philippians 2:1–3 says: "If you have any encouragement from being united with Christ, if any comfort from His love, if any fellowship with the Spirit, if any tenderness and compassion, then make my joy complete by being like minded, having the same love, being one in spirit and purpose. Do nothing out of selfish ambition or vain conceit, but in humility consider others better than yourselves."

## ABOUT THE AUTHOR

Barbara Rosberg is the cohost of the national daily call-in radio program, *America's Family Coaches—Live*. An established and sought-after speaker, she coauthored *The 5 Love Needs of Men and Women* and wrote *Divorce-Proof Your Marriage*. She has a passion for teaching women how to meet their husband's needs while also understanding their own God-given needs. She challenges and shows women how to make their marriages great, avoiding the suffering that comes from painful or difficult marital relations. She and Gary have been married for nearly thirty years, have raised two daughters, and have one grandson.

## VERSES THAT INSPIRE

Love is patient, love is kind. It does not envy, it does not boast, it is not proud. It is not rude, it is not self-seeking, it is not easily angered, it keeps no record of wrongs. Love does not delight in evil but rejoices with the truth. It always protects, always trusts, always hopes, always perseveres. (1 Corinthians 13:4–7)

Since you have purified your souls in obeying the truth through the Spirit in sincere love of the brethren, love one another fervently with a pure heart. (1 Peter 1:22 NKJV)

You too are being built together to become a dwelling in which God lives by his Spirit. (Ephesians 2:22)

# Can God Heal a Marriage?

DEB LAASER

*Do not conform any longer to the pattern of this world,*
*but be transformed by the renewing of your mind.*
*Then you will be able to test and approve what God's will is—*
*his good, pleasing and perfect will.*

—ROMANS 12:2

## THE BEGINNING OF BROKENNESS

During the first fifteen years of our marriage, Mark and I realized that the annoyances of life were always slipping in.

There were many wonderful things about our love and our family; however, there never seemed to be enough time, money, patience or connection for our coupleship. We were slowly drifting apart, but it was so gradual that I don't think we even realized it at first. As a pastor and a counselor, Mark always seemed to be the one people needed, wanted, and admired, and his life of being publicly cherished created huge resentment and loneliness for me. I was sinking into hopelessness, thinking that something was definitely missing.

Today I can see that it was extraordinary how God's hand was in so many of the circumstances that followed. What was also extraordinary was how He could take a very ordinary woman like me and walk me through an incredible journey of growth and transformation. He has provided hope when there was no hope. He has provided healing when my heart was reeling with pain. He has given me skills to develop authentic relationships with my children, my friends, my employees, my husband, and with Him. He has provided intimacy in my marriage that is beyond my wildest dreams. What is extraordinary is that He loved me enough to take my hand and lead me to the right places and the right people to find His extraordinary love in all of my life. I had no idea that He could love me that much.

One day two of Mark's colleagues from his clinic came home with him and asked to talk with me. Despair was filling the room and I knew that it was not going to be good news. The four of us sat in the living room. For the first time, I was told of some of Mark's sinful sexual behaviors. They talked matter-of-factly as they informed me that he was a sexual pervert, that they had fired him, and that they were sorry. These informants were not just casual coworkers. One of them was a therapist and the other was a medical doctor who was raised on the mission field. They were friends. And yet, in this moment of fear for their clinic and their inexperience with sexual addiction, even they could not offer much comfort or hope. It is truly one of the darkest, loneliest days I can ever remember.

As only God can provide, I also felt a huge sense of relief in those hours that followed. Maybe this could somehow explain why I couldn't grasp that "something more" in my marriage. Maybe this was why on the outside we looked liked we had a wonderful marriage and family, but on the inside, I was often lonely and resentful. In those dark hours I know the Holy Spirit was with us. The brokenness that I witnessed in Mark as I saw him slouched in our navy blue wing chair was beyond words. The calm that came over me to make a decision to stay and listen and try to support him was not of me.

The days that followed were like a whirlwind. A board member and recovering alcoholic from Mark's clinic knew of a treatment center in Minneapolis for sexual addiction. He said that there was help and hope as he knew that sex addiction was very much like alcoholism. He helped Mark get connected there, and within three days, Mark was leaving for a thirty-day in-patient program. It was expensive and we had no means to pay, but this wonderful physician agreed to take care of it for Mark—in full. The grace of God had only begun.

I'm not sure how I managed those weeks. We lived in a fairly small town and the information about Mark's behaviors was front-page news. The public humiliation drove me into isolation with embarrassment and shame I had never experienced. I had no one to talk to other than Mary, my business partner. I did not know of support groups. Friends, church members, and colleagues all stayed away. I had three small children to care for and no financial means to do so. I needed to be strong, but on the inside, I was terrified.

Family week was a treatment center tradition where spouses and other family members were invited to join in the therapeutic process. During family week, my recovery officially began. I went there to support Mark and to do whatever I needed to do to help him get better. I was filled with information about family systems. I began to understand that we are products of whom we live with and how we do relationships together. Mark and I met with therapists and processed in groups about our experiences. We journaled, we shared stories, we cried—and for the first time, we began to experience a closeness in sharing our hearts. This was what I was missing. I knew it. This closeness was beginning out of brokenness and adversity. This was being vulnerable and intimate—how different this was from my original fantasy that having happiness would provide closeness.

When Mark's stay at the treatment center ended, there were lots of decisions about what aftercare would be. Therapy appointments and groups were arranged for both of us back home—but I wasn't convinced that I needed weekly therapy too. It only took one session with my therapist, Maureen, to convince me that I was in the right place doing the right thing. I know today that God brought me to this wise and gentle woman to lead me down a path of self-awareness and transformation that has changed my life.

This intense therapy lasted eighteen months or so—until we moved to Minneapolis for Mark's new job. Mark and I met weekly in therapy-led support groups—I was in a women's group and Mark was in a men's group. At the same time, we participated in a couple's group. Additionally, we both took time for individual sessions in therapy and went to twelve-step groups. My bedside table was stacked with recovery books and I began my addiction to tapes. I could not get enough information. I was alive for the first time in my life, even though there were weeks and months of much grieving and sadness. As I

*As I learned how to create support around me, I knew that I could be safe to deal with great sadness and anger.*

learned how to create support around me, I knew that I could be safe to deal with great sadness and anger.

After months of recovery, we began to envision a new beginning and to plan for the move to Minneapolis. And then the other shoe dropped. The doorbell rang and a policeman in full uniform handed me an envelope. It was a lawsuit. I couldn't imagine how I could endure anything more. I was shaken to the core and terrified for Mark. The media loved the news. It seemed as if the whole world was watching. I would have rather died that day. Actually, the "shoes" kept coming, and before it was all over, three lawsuits were filed. For a couple of years we lived in the ambiguity of those court decisions and what they would do to us financially. I vascillated between anger and compassion and hopelessness. I felt like I was on a roller coaster of emotions that would never stop.

Mark was devoted to the endless needs of starting a new career, but it was evident that he was willing to do whatever it took to stay faithful and true to our marriage and to his recovery. I am humbled sometimes to admit that I was not nearly as motivated to keep working so hard at recovery. I wanted to be "normal" and not carry the label of a sexually addicted family. Depletion of time, energy, and resources can easily creep into the demise of any effort to heal from sexual addiction. When at least one of us has been able to lead and encourage the other through those times, we have begun to witness the strength of our one-flesh union. God has taught us that both husband and wife don't need to be strong (or healthy) at the same time. That is why He makes us companions. If one stumbles and falls, the other is there to be supportive. I admit that there were numerous times when I wanted to run from it all. I had had enough of talking about sex! We really did work on lots of other issues, but there were days when I thought that all we dealt with was addiction.

My personal journey continued in lots of ordinary ways. From seminars to women's tennis leagues, I was spending time getting to know and cherish some of the dormant parts of my life. In doing so, I came more and more alive to my relationships with Mark and others. Transformation was happening in many little ways each day and would continue for the rest of my life.

## WHAT IS TRANSFORMATION?

The first step to transforming my marriage was making a decision to stay. Despite the dishonesty, the betrayal, and the broken vows, I chose to stay. When I made that transforming decision, it was important for me to claim that I didn't need to stay, but that I wanted to stay. I was capable of taking care of myself. I was not making a decision to stay married simply because I needed a roof over my head and someone to provide for our three small children. I was making a conscious decision to participate in my marriage. I was making a decision to be just as accountable for what I brought to our marriage. I wanted to be an equal partner in exploring and sharing our lives, to be weak sometimes or strong sometimes, knowing that both contributed to the strength of our marriage. I needed to stop keeping score about whose behavior was more sinful and accept the fact that we both did hurtful, sinful things. There came a day when I knew that I could still be angry, sad, or frightened (and that Mark was willing to listen to all of that), but that I was going to stay.

The second step in transforming my thinking was accepting the fact that sexual addiction was not the cause of our marital problem. We both brought all of the elements to our marriage to create distance. We had no idea how to be close emotionally. We knew how to do life together—get through school, have sex, find jobs, have kids, fix up houses, get involved in the community—but we were failing at sharing our feelings and being vulnerable with each other. Sexual addiction was only one of the symptoms of the infection that was growing in our relationship. We were simply unable to be emotionally present for each other.

Coping with the loneliness and anger in his life, Mark looked for love and nurturing primarily through sex, which led to his sexual acting out. The predisposition for that kind of behavior was established by the wounds he experienced as a boy. When he stopped his sexual sin, he still had all of those needs. I had also had ways of "acting out" my loneliness. I withdrew. I became silent. I used passive-aggression to live happily with others around me but cut Mark out of my life. I poured myself into my children's lives with love I could not seem to give to Mark. I kept busy with endless chores and projects around the house. And I always had my business to provide the excitement, creativity and connection with others that I so desperately wanted with Mark. I, too, choose ways to cope. I, too, had wounds from my past. In order to understand and make different choices about my behaviors, I needed to examine and heal from some of those. My behaviors were more socially acceptable things to do than sexually acting out, so it was easy for me to put my issues on the back burner and keep the focus and blame on Mark. As I finally embraced the fact that I contributed in my own way to the ineffective cycles of connecting with Mark, then I could see transformation beginning.

When I came to those first two places of transformation—deciding to stay and deciding to look at myself—I was ready for a deeper relationship with God.

## THE THREE ACTS OF SURRENDER

Mark and I have come to see that for us to really transform our marriage into a one-flesh union, there are three essential acts of surrender:

1. *I really needed to surrender my life to Christ.* When Mark and I crashed from the adversity of sexual addiction, I couldn't imagine dealing with greater adversities. I had spoken "the first three steps" at many meetings: I admitted that I was powerless over my life, that I believed in a power greater than myself, and that I made a decision to turn my life over to God. As much as I would like to admit that I really lived that way, it actually took several more adversities before I feel to my knees and fully understood this act of surrender.

As my children grew into young adults, I realized that all of my recovery-oriented parenting could not prevent them for experiencing some of the loneliness, brokenness, despair, and unhealthy choices in their lives. I was powerless. I had to surrender them to God.

I met Pam, who not only became the perfect employee, but also my spiritual mentor, supporter, and believer in me as a leader. When I knew I needed to find more balance in my life, she was the one I chose to train to delegate many of my business responsibilities. But then Pam was diagnosed with pancreatic cancer and died within seven months. I experienced my powerlessness again. I could see clearly that my way was once again not God's way. My best efforts to control my life were just that—my efforts. I needed to surrender.

And then my company began backsliding after seventeen years of growth. It had provided financially for our family for many years and nourished my creative and leadership skills. At first my partner and I excused our faltering on the typical worldly things. But after a while, I clearly began to realize that my dreams were not God's dreams for me and I surrendered slowly the vision of my life's work. It was clear that God was making way for His greater plans. I needed to surrender.

In all of these and other shattered dreams of mine, I began to see God's joy in my life. I was devastated by so many losses and was crying out for some assurance that God had not forsaken me. The book *Shattered Dreams* by Larry Crabb was His personal word of comfort when I was reeling with the pain. I kept looking for happiness everywhere. And sometimes I would find it. But true joy was quite different; it was much more profound and long-lasting. Really letting go was the key. Not just asking for relief or some partial fix to problems, but really disbanding my ability to even have answers or abilities to do anything—being willing to do anything with whatever resources I was given for His plan. I surrendered myself to Christ.

2. *I needed to surrender Mark to Christ.* By that I simply learned that I could not guarantee his staying and loving me. I could not control his acting out or his willingness to be totally honest with me. I could decide to trust again, but really, trust is built upon consistent behavior each and every day—and I really could not control that either. I could not know for sure that I knew every detail of his behavior, and at some point, I had to surrender that need to know over to God. I needed to turn Mark's life over to Christ and to trust that if we worked at loving each other the way He loves us, He would find a way to restore the intimacy that we desired.

3. *I turned the dreams that I had of our marriage over to Christ.* There were many of those fantasies: being taken care of by my "hero," having successful careers, being perfect parents, having money to do whatever we wanted to do, being leaders in our church. When the tragedy of sexual addiction and subsequent losses hit our lives, it was easy to stay stuck in the grieving of a life that was "wasted." After years of fight-

ing to get back what I thought I had lost, I surrendered our marriage to God in great anticipation of what He would chose for us to do. The new vision that He has been putting in place is incredible. He is winding our two lives together in ministry for His hurting people and using our pain for that purpose. The life I had been trying to hide from because of all the pain was becoming the one He wanted to use! It was time to surrender.

## THE SEVEN DESIRES OF THE HEART

The next order of transformation for us has been understanding each other's needs and how to truly be each other's servant in them.

I had come to my wedding with many needs for Mark to fulfill. I wasn't very lighthearted, so I needed him to be funny. I wasn't very outgoing, so I loved that he loved people. I wasn't very comfortable with sex, so it was terrific that he was. I longed for a more spiritual life, so it was perfect that Mark was going into the ministry. I worked hard to understand and find healing for myself with all of these issues so that our coupleship was not merely for the purpose of fulfilling my incompleteness. I have also come to find that during this time, Mark needed me to be certain things for him too. We were both expecting each other to complete each other in all the wrong ways.

Today, I know that we do complete each other if we can minister to some very basic desires that we both have. I know that we have all the differences that men and women have, but at the core of our soul, we have a lot in common. No matter how imperfect our pasts were, we would still have these "desires of our heart."

The first "desire of the heart is to be *heard*. When I can exprees a feeling or a need, I feel attended to and nurtured when I am heard. In my family, my parents were very loving, but we rarely talked about emotional issues. There were times when I was lonely, confused, or hurting and didn't know who to talk to. So I learned to be quiet. I couldn't really expect Mark or anyone else to "hear me" until I first learned how to talk about my feelings and needs. I brought years of wanting to be heard and understood into our marriage.

Another desire is to feel *physically safe*. We need to feel safe with each other so that we can be vulnerable with each other. I discovered that I really needed Mark to provide for us, to be the leader in our marriage. I also found that it has been better to encourage him than to criticize him. When we do that for each other, we begin to see how our coupleship works as a "team."

The next desire that we have is to be *affirmed*—I have a need to be appreciated for things I do and who I am. Many women stress themselves out trying to do things for everyone else just so they can feel affirmed. Likewise, I need to be affirming. I discovered that Mark was longing for the very same kind words from me.

I also desire to be *praised*—to be loved just because I am! Sometimes I want Mark just to be glad that I'm around, to smile when he sees me coming into the room, and to tell me he's glad I'm there. I found out that for Mark, too, a lot of what he did was due to his need to find praise somewhere. Today, we work really hard at affirming and praising each other.

Another desire is to be *touched*. From the time we are

babies until we die, we need touch. Unfortunately, many couples don't know how to give that to each other without some kind of sexual connotation. That was true for Mark. He desperately wanted to be touched, but he didn't know how to express his need. He had to work really hard to let me know that all he wanted was to hold my hand or hug me and that it wasn't about sex. I have found that getting touched in this way has freed me up to be aware of my own sexuality. When all we did as a couple was get into the pattern of Mark always initiating and me always defending, it didn't allow either of us to really enjoy touch. Touch is a need to warmly connect, not just to be sexual.

I have a desire to be *passionately desired*—to be the one and only love of Mark's life. All of us, including Mark, just want to be the only person in our spouse's life. In our current sexually obsessed culture, we do so many things to be "desirable." We have learned that desire for each other is so much more than sexual. We desire each other emotionally and spiritually. We want to be each other's best friend. There are things that only we share, including all the events of a thirty-year marriage.

Finally, I have a desire to be *included*—to feel wanted and invited in the significant arenas of Mark's world. Since I was a little girl, I wanted to be a part of someone's life. I seek relationship, with God and with others. Neither one of us needs to be off just doing "our own thing." We both have our own lives, gifts, and talents, but today we seek to include each other in all that we do.

As we have been able to minister to each other's basic desires of the heart, our intimacy has grown and we have seen our relationship transformed!

We know that we have cycles of reacting to each other. When Mark does something that triggers me, I respond in a certain way. He may not even know that he is doing it. It can be so many symbolic things that remind me of various pains from the past. I go back to being like a wounded girl. I get quiet and distant. My response then triggers him to feel lost and abandoned. And we begin the dance of distancing from each other and trying to figure out how to medicate our frustration, loneliness, or anger. If we dissect the places where we get stuck, we can always find a desire of the heart that needs to be nurtured. We know that we cannot always be the one to love perfectly or provide companionship continually. We have learned how to reach out to healthy behaviors and people to fulfill those desires in those times. But our choice as we move toward greater transformation is to be soul mates as much as possible.

## ALLOWING MY PAIN TO BE THE PAIN

In the first weeks and months of acknowledging the huge and hurtful issues of my husband's sexual addiction, my pain seemed to almost break my heart. Literally, it is a feeling that I will never forget. I cried for months. I grieved for many more wondering how I would ever recover from the shame and loss in my life. I isolated myself as best as I could because I thought that surely people would not want to associate with me. I was full of pity and confusion and hopelessness.

Out of all of those feelings came life for me. I have been transformed into a new woman, a more loving wife, a better mom, a more compassionate boss, and a more generous and understanding friend. It has taken me too long, perhaps, to see that God uses this pain to connect me to others in pain. It has been in my brokenness that I have been able to accept love and to give love. It is in my weakness that I have known what God's love is all about and that I have been ultimately able to surrender my life to Him. It is in this opportunity to grow from the pain that I have now claimed the fruits of His spirit to be mine: love, joy, peace, patience, kindness, goodness, faithfulness, gentleness, and self-control (Galatians 5:22–23).

In Matthew 11:28–30, Jesus said that all of us who are weary should come to Him. Then He says we should take on His yoke and burden. I never liked that part much, but today I understand it. Just as God was willing to become a man and experience all of our pain and sin, my pain is the way that I can connect with God and with others. My pain is the pain of all humanity. There are so many of us who struggle in so many of the same ways. If we would only surrender to Christ and share our pain despite our fears of what others might think, we would find that we grow closer. When I had my "normal" life years ago, I was lonely. Since I have allowed myself to embrace my pain, I have known an intimacy with God and others that I never knew before. I would have never known the fullness of life if I had not had shattered dreams. I also know that God will forever love me, guide me, and provide for me if only I let Him do that. His blessings continue to flow in far greater abundance than I could have ever desired.

## ABOUT THE AUTHOR

After twenty-five years of running her own business, Deb Laaser has joined her husband Mark in their ministry. Through Faithful and True Ministries she teaches, speaks, writes, and counsels on sexual integrity. Deb and Mark's personal journey of recovery from sexual infidelity began in 1987 and has provided them with experiences and hope that they share with others who struggle with this issue. The Laasers have three children.

## VERSES THAT INSPIRE

Because of the LORD's great love we are not consumed, for his compassions never fail. They are new every morning; great is your faithfulness. (Lamentations 3:22–23)

May the God of hope fill you with all joy and peace as you trust in him, so that you may overflow with hope by the power of the Holy Spirit. (Romans 15:13)

God is our refuge and strength, an ever-present help in trouble. (Psalm 46:1)

No eye has seen, no ear has heard, no mind has conceived what God has prepared for those who love him. (1 Corinthians 2:9)

I love the LORD, for he heard my voice;

he heard my cry for mercy. . . .

I was overcome by trouble and sorrow.

Then I called on the name of the LORD:

"O LORD, save me!"

The LORD is gracious and righteous;

our God is full of compassion.

The LORD protects the simplehearted;

when I was in great need, he saved me.

(Psalm 116:1, 3–6)

Blessed is the man who perseveres under trial, because when he has stood the test, he will receive the crown of life that God has promised to those who love him. (James 1:12)

# Talk, Touch, and Tenderness in Marriage

❧

CARRIE OLIVER

*An excellent wife is the crown of her husband, but she who*

*causes shame is like rottenness in his bones.*

—PROVERBS 12:4 NKJV

In the beginning God created the world, and He took great joy in His creation. Then He decided to create man and woman. "So God created man in his own image, in the image of God he created him; male and female he created them" (Genesis 1:27). Later we read more details about why and how God created woman. "It is not good for the man to be alone. I will make a helper suitable for him" (Genesis 2:18). Thus God made woman to have a relationship with man—to become one, to be his helper. Since the beginning of time when God declared all that he made "good," He established marriage to be the ultimate relationship between two people. Even so, we don't have to look too far to see that what God once declared as good has deteriorated. Good things are just not happening in many marital relationships.

Most women wish they had a closer relationship with their husband. They yearn to be understood, to share their feelings, to be appreciated, and to feel close to someone emotionally. There's a great story that I love to tell that illustrates this.

There once was a husband who felt his wife didn't understand everything he had to deal with in his job, so he prayed and asked God to change their roles as husband and wife. Well, sure enough God heard his prayer and the next morning he woke up as his wife, and she had turned into him.

He kissed her good-bye and she went off to his job, and he eagerly began his day as the wife. He cooked breakfast for the kids and assembled their backpacks complete with sack lunches. He loaded them into the minivan, picked up the carpool kids, and took them all to school. Then he ran a number of errands. He stopped by the cleaners and the bank, then the power and telephone companies. Following that, he shopped for groceries, took them home, unloaded them all, and put them away. Next, he separated the laundry into whites and colors and began several loads of wash.

After that he made the beds, vacuumed, dusted, and swept and mopped the floors. Before he knew it, it was time to pick the kids up from school. He drove downtown, loaded the kids into the car, and settled arguments on the way home. Back at the house, he prepared them a snack, then sat them down to do their homework while he began dinner.

In the meantime, his wife returned home from his job, sat down in his favorite overstuffed chair, and read the sports page. When dinner was ready, the family sat down and had a lovely meal together. The husband cleaned up the dishes, orchestrated showers, and put the kids to bed. By this time, he was exhausted! And even though he had not completed all of the things that his wife typically completed in a day, he was ready to go to sleep. So he crawled into bed, thankful to be getting some rest. But in the midst of this dramatic change that he had prayed for, his wife received all the testosterone that he once had, so he did not really go to sleep as soon as he had wanted!

The next morning when he woke up, he fell to his knees and asked God to switch him and his wife back to their original roles.

"Well," God said in response to his request, "I would be glad to do that. And if you can wait nine months, I will. But the thing is, you became pregnant last night."

While women might laugh at the exaggeration of this story, if we're honest we'd have to admit that we've secretly harbored that fantasy ourselves. It's not just the duties or struggles we wish our mates would understand, but we wish he would know our feelings, have some insight into what makes us tick, and realize how much we long for a deeper level of intimacy with him.

Women across America would love to have a better marriage—a better relationship with their spouse. Yet two-thirds of all divorces in the U.S. are filed by women. A recent *Time* magazine article pointed out that more women are making decisions to leave their marriages because they are becoming increasingly lonely and unfulfilled. Furthermore, these women believe that marriage is not going to give them what they need, so they're either ending the relationship or looking elsewhere to get their needs met.

Regardless of statistics or your situation, it is possible to experience greater fulfillment in your marriage. You don't have to settle for mediocrity or second-best. You can begin right now to change your perspective and experience the kind of relationship God intended you and your husband to have.

## STEPS TO GREATER INTIMACY

The typical married woman falls into one of three categories:

1. You are fairly pleased with your marriage relationship, but you have a sense that maybe it could be better. You would like to see you and your husband communicate better and also handle conflict in more constructive ways.

2. You aren't very excited about your marriage right now. You've tried a few things to improve your relationship, but there's been no significant change.

3. You're ready to give up. You're convinced you've tried everything. You've attended marriage seminars, read marriage manuals, and even attended counseling. You've tried a weekly date night and even made an effort to enter into his world by doing some of the activities he enjoys. But after all these attempts, you're still feeling lonely and tired, disconnected and alone.

If you find yourself in category three, I have a special word of encouragement for you. According to research, not only can good marriages go bad, but bad marriages can also go good. In 1988, 13,000 couples were asked to rate their marriage on a scale from very unhappy to very happy. Five years later, the couples who rated their marriage very unhappy but still stayed together had now become the 86 percent who said their marriage was now either happy or very happy.

Almost every woman I have met has desired greater intimacy with her husband. This desire is a God-given need in all of us. Naturally, it is tempting to look elsewhere and imagine our need being met; however, regardless of where we turn—another man, food, or shopping—they will all leave

us unsatisfied. This is because God designed us to find fulfillment in our marriage. Here are some simple steps to help
you make a fresh connection with your husband, thus result-
ing in greater intimacy and a more fulfilling marriage.

## STEP ONE: CULTIVATE DEEPER INTIMACY WITH GOD

First, renew your overall perspective by cultivating a deeper
level of intimacy with God. When we become discouraged
with our husbands, we tend to focus on the problem. When
this occurs, it's difficult to see any constructive solution. We
all know that our relationship with God is important, and
yet the pain and disillusionment in our marriage can often
distract us from the inner strength God gave us to maintain
an intimacy with Him. Ask yourself, when was the last time
you encountered God so deeply that your life was changed in
some way?

An encounter that I will always remember took place
when I was in my last year at Denver Seminary. Like most
graduate students, I saved all my difficult classes for the last
year of school. In one of them, I was assigned to write a

research paper on the Sermon on the Mount. Fortunately, my husband has an extensive library, so I perused his books and discovered Dr. Martin Lloyd Jones's two-volume series titled *The Sermon on the Mount.* As I sat down to gather research, I gave some thought to Dr. Jones's words about what it means to be broken, a situation I had never really considered in my relationship with God. While I wrote the paper God nudged me to consider what it means to hunger and thirst after righteousness and what it means to have a heart that is pure.

Initially I thought I was going to write a research paper on the Sermon on the Mount, but God forced me to look at the Beatitudes in order to change my attitude in the area of relationships. The Beatitude prayers became a conduit between God and me that cultivated in my having a desire for Him. When we have intimacy with our Maker, our prayer life becomes transformed and our worship experience with Him deepens. When we choose to change our perspective and cultivate an increased intimacy with God, we'll begin to recognize His presence in our life in new and powerful ways.

God did not design us to be stagnant creatures. We were formed to grow, change, and become like Him. This process is called sanctification. Now if you're thinking, *I'm not the one who needs to change, but rather my husband,* then perhaps you are not open to change. If that's the case, you're not going to grow, and if you don't grow, you'll wither up inside and die emotionally and spiritually. The growth

> *God did not design us to be stagnant creatures. We were formed to grow, change, and become like Him.*

process begins with our relationship with Jesus and then continues in our other relationships with our spouse, our children, and our friends.

## BARRIERS THAT HINDER CHANGE

There are, however, several barriers that can prevent you from growing and changing:

1. *You feel like a failure.* Perhaps an experience from the past has made you feel terribly disappointed. It prevents you from moving on and growing. You often feel "stuck."

2. *You struggle with the need to control.* You're organized and structured, but what prevents you from changing and growing is your need to impose your structure and organization on other people in your life. A strong need to control extends into your feelings, and you do not allow God to enter your emotional process. Everything in your life is so controlled, it prevents growth.

3. *You have a problem with pride.* Pride claims, "It's everybody else's fault!" Remember the old saying: "When you point at someone else, there are three fingers pointing back at yourself." Focusing on the shortcomings of others cultivates our pride and we exalt ourselves further, which hampers growth.

4. *You struggle with selfishness.* You want your own way and fail to see the needs of others. Pride and selfishness often go hand in hand. When we focus on "I," we become consumed with our own needs—often refusing or reluctantly fulfilling the needs of others. This can leave you feeling lonely and unhappy because your focus becomes yourself, rather than Christ or others.

5. *You are insecure.* As a result, you make everybody else

in your life responsible for your happiness. This places a lot of pressure on others, since no one except Christ can fulfill all your needs. We initially expect others to attain perfection, which only sets them up to fail. And when they do let us down (because they will), we are devastated. Remaining here in this cycle will not permit growth; it cultivates stagnation.

6. *You have unresolved anger and bitterness.* It's okay to be angry, but if you don't uncover the source of the anger, it will ultimately result in bitterness. When you are bitter, your heart is incapable of being compassionate or forgiving. When this occurs, you remain focused on perceived injustices to self, with little energy for repairing your marriage.

Change is difficult and can be painful. But a different kind of pain occurs when we cease to change the way God wants us to. Ultimately, we will experience far more suffering if we sidestep necessary growing pains. But when we are committed to growth, we remain open to God's transforming power in our lives. The result? We release the need to change others, which allows us to focus on God's work in us. And when you allow God to work in you, no matter what happens in your marriage, you can stand before God and know that you have, first and foremost, been accountable to Him.

In my own marriage, God altered me in ways I never thought possible before I pressed through the discomfort of change. He softened my heart to allow me to see things in a new and fresh way. I urge you to cultivate an intimacy with your Lord, Jesus Christ. He is the beginning of every relationship and the reason we exist.

## STEP TWO: REDEFINE YOUR RELATIONSHIP WITH YOUR HUSBAND

Step number two is to redefine your relationship with your mate. This requires a new perspective, an "attitude adjustment" toward your husband, which will allow you to see him in a different light. When we lose hope, our perspective becomes distorted and it's easy to develop a critical spirit. In his book *Seven Principles for Making Marriage Work,* John Gottman cites research that shows a major predictor of divorce is when a couple's negative interactions outweigh the positive. Conversely, when we are focused on what is good, right, and helpful in our marriage, it draws a couple closer and promotes a positive relationship. It is not always easy to see your husband through a new lens. It involves letting go of past mistakes that may require forgiveness, but it can give value to your relationship in new and revitalizing ways.

In both my counseling practice and my home, I like to use the technique called the "as-if principle." How this works is that we treat people in our lives, such as our husbands, as if they already have the attributes we want them to have. We treat them as if they are good communicators. We look at them and expect them to be good listeners. We consider them to be good friends. We treat them as if they genuinely care about the relationship. When we use the as-if principle with people we know, they begin to rise to the level of these attributes over a period of time. Conversely, when we treat people negatively, they tend to give up on themselves or the relationship, possibly falling below the standard we set for them.

Perhaps you have a negative perspective of your husband. Maybe he's said or done things that have harmed you on a consistent basis, and although you have forgiven him, you still live with the residual effects of a damaged heart. What can you do to overcome this perspective? Accept and embrace the fact that he is actually different from you. Men handle things completely differently than women. There are literally hundreds of books on the market that explain the differences. We expect our mates to respond to circumstances the way we would. When they don't, we develop a negative outlook on them. We think, *If he really loves me, he'll do this,* and when he doesn't, we feed our negativity with the fuel of failed expectations. Keep in mind that *different* is defined as "being distinct." But we construe *different* to mean *wrong.* We forget that God made our husbands much different from us. In fact, *intimacy* is actually defined as two separate people coming together as one; it is not two people becoming the same. And yet frequently we want to mold and shape our spouse to look like us. This approach will bring failure. Our mate naturally resists conforming to our likeness because it's not who he is. God had something much different in mind for him.

In my early years with Gary, I never considered our differences as male and female. When conflicts arose from those particular differences, I spent a lot of time focusing on how he needed to change what he did that was wrong. Then God, in His infinite wisdom, gave me three sons, which forced me to accept the differences I had struggled against with other males in my life. Since I only have two sisters, I did not enter marriage with a lot of insight into the drastic differences between men and women. Even though all people share some similarities, on the whole we're quite different. Consider, for example, this quote from Gary's and my book, *Raising Sons and Loving It*:

> Here are some common misperceptions that women might have of men. Men don't share feelings or emotions. Men seem to go into a trance when they're watching sports or when certain subjects are brought up like they can't handle more than one subject at a time. Men seem to think that they can do better even when they can't. Men need more sensitivity, concern, compassion, and empathy. Men are so involved with their work and career, they want a family but they don't really want to get involved. Do they think about anything but sex?

Well, men have their own set of common complaints about women. Women are too emotional. They need to be more logical. Women are too sensitive, always getting their feelings hurt. Women are so changeable, we wish they would make up their minds. Maybe women think we can read minds, but actually, we can't. And so what's wrong with a sex drive anyway? Women think they have a spiritual gift of changing men. Women are so involved with other people and their problems. Actually, women are moody and negative. You just can't satisfy them.

When a couple learns that such frustrations are normal responses to gender differences, they can then begin to accept each other rather than attempt to change each other. A recent article stated that women might be less happy in their marriages because a wife comes to the relationship with a whole lot of different expectations than her husband does. And one of the biggest expectations is that her husband wants the same kind of relationship that she does. The truth is, rarely do men do anything the way we do.

They don't engage in friendships the way we do, they don't communicate like we do; in fact, they do very few things like we do.

For most women, relationships are of great value. I've learned that just because I value relationship does not mean that I will define how it works for everyone else who is involved. As a result, when I think about my relationship with Gary, I think about it in new ways. We are beginning to rewrite a definition of our relationship and our "coupleness."

## INSIGHT INTO THE MIND OF MEN

The following insights into men will help you rethink your relationship. On the whole, men are achievement-oriented, solution-focused, and goal-oriented. This does not mean that a woman can't have goals or be competitive or enjoy success. But most women do not derive their sense of self-esteem from these kinds of things like men do.

So when your husband comes home from work or you have a chance to talk, don't ask him how he felt about his day, but ask him if he achieved the things he set out to do that day. Or before he goes to work, ask him what his goals are for that day. In this way, you are speaking to him in a language he knows well. When you do this, you will begin to discover a new and fresh way to connect with him.

Men are also more apt to communicate information rather than feelings. In fact, men usually withdraw when faced with feelings, especially if they are centered on conflict. This probably comes as no surprise to a married woman. But you still want to share your feelings with your husband and hear his feelings as well. However, you need to avoid overwhelming your husband with a wide variety of feelings—while your best friend can handle it, your husband may be at a loss as to how to react. For example, when you tell him, "The phone has not stopped ringing, this house is a mess, the kids are driving me crazy, I'm going nuts, and I'm not sure I can make it through the rest of the day," he may have trouble processing all those feelings and experiences at one time. Instead, exchange one feeling at a time with him such as "I'm sad," or "I'm frustrated." Also, keep in mind (because he is solution-focused and goal-oriented) that he's going to want to remedy your problems. Let him know ahead of time that you just want him to listen. Of course, he may stand there and not know how to react. Sometimes if I'm feeling sad, I might ask my husband to pray for me. Or if I'm feeling over-whelmed, I might ask him to run an errand. But I stick to one feeling at a time and then I ask him to do something that will help me. In this way, I've communicated my feelings, but in a way that is more suitable to him.

Another area of intimacy that would mean a great deal to women is to have their husband share his feelings. How-ever, husbands, and men in general, do not focus on how they're feeling during the day. We need to keep this in mind. Consider this quote from *Raising Sons*, as it pertains to a man and his emotions:

Wives who want to understand their husbands emotionally should probably give up hoping that they'll accomplish this through long, leisurely hours of talking about feelings. Don't push your husband to talk about his feelings. If you bring up the subject of his feelings and he doesn't respond, maybe at that time, it's a good time to drop it. You can make your husband actually feel pressured or uncomfortable with the subject of asking him if he wants to talk about his feelings. Let him know that it's okay if he doesn't want to talk at that point.

In the years I've been married, I've noticed that when Gary is going through an emotional situation he often becomes withdrawn. He needs space. Instead of asking him about his feelings or asking if there's anything I can do, I leave him alone. Then when he seems to come around, I use that opportunity to try to connect with him. I might ask him if he's okay or to tell me what he was struggling with or if God had guided him in any particular direction. But I try to dwell on the process rather than on his feelings. And as I do, I listen to what he tells me. He may never openly share an emotion, but I discern an undercurrent of feelings as he shares with me in a manner that is comfortable for him.

## STEP THREE: REINVEST IN YOUR HUSBAND

The third step is to reinvest in your husband by choosing to relate to him in ways he finds meaningful.

Almost every couple I see in counseling wants to relate to one another in healthier and more intimate ways. Here are some effective ways of nourishing and loving your husband that will relate to him in a meaningful manner.

1. *Acknowledge and encourage him.* After I've worked with a couple for a few weeks and we've defined their individual needs, I'll ask the husband, "Have you been working on the changes that your wife suggested?" He'll inevitably say, "Yes, I've been trying to make some changes." And when I ask the wife, "Have you noticed his changes, and are you encouraging him as he makes them?", she'll often say, "No, I haven't." I'm always surprised at this response, but then I look at myself and remember that I also forget to be an encourager. I become so focused on my daily tasks and the problems that

> *In addition to verbalizing your love, observe your husband in order to understand what personally communicates love to him.*

have come up, that I forget to add a positive note to the end of the day.

2. *Communicate your love to him in ways that will make*

*him feel loved.* In addition to verbalizing your love, observe your husband in order to understand what personally communicates love to him. Gary feels loved when I listen to his ideas and dreams. In the early years of our marriage, I would discourage him by saying, "We can't possibly go on that trip or we can't do that or that's a strange idea." You see, I'm much more of a here-and-now type of person. I don't project into the future very often; yet he thrives on dreaming. I eventually learned that the one thing that says love to him is when I sit and listen and allow him to envision his dreams. More than once I've been surprised at how exciting his ideas are.

Another thing that demonstrates my love for Gary is when I support him in his parenting. This has probably been one of the greatest areas of conflict in our marriage. When I stopped suggesting ways for him to parent, God showed me that I was never going to be a father to our sons, because He'd given that role to Gary. Rather than interfere at inappropriate times, I've learned to support him as he makes parenting decisions, which translates as love to him.

Gary also enjoys time alone every once in a while, so I demonstrate my love for him when I leave him alone and don't interfere. Additionally, he enjoys it when I listen to his oldies songs without criticizing them or calling them goofy! One thing he also really enjoys is my accompanying him when he scuba dives. It's been a challenge, because I don't really like to be in deep water with a tank strapped on my back. But you need to think about your husband. What might be a sacrifice that would communicate your love to him? Study him for clues. Understand what makes him tick and "speak" to him in ways that suit his love language.

3. *Practice the power of forgiveness.* Early on in our marriage I was great at saying I was sorry. As I look back, however, I really wanted harmony rather than restoration at that time. Seeking forgiveness is a matter of the heart, purposely turning away from a specific infraction and making the promise not to inflict harm in that way again. It's not something you simply do for the sake of restoring peace.

True forgiveness does not say, "I was wrong, but you . . ." God will give you the strength to admit your failures and mistakes, if you turn to Him. Consider these nine words: "I was wrong. I am sorry. Please forgive me." It is a crucial moment when we cease to focus on our husband's wrongs and instead look at our own. It may be at that point that we release our pride and learn to forgive.

Many of you still might ask the question, "Will I ever experience what I first signed up for when I married my husband?" You expected closeness, a friend, a companion, and intimacy. I believe most husbands want these things as well. Nobody enters into matrimony to be miserable. You might be thinking, *Do I have to do everything in this relationship?* But let me ask you this: How successful have you been at changing your husband into someone you want him to be? If your marriage needs a shot in the arm, don't wait for him to make it happen. Focus on the person you can change—you. Consider Psalm 139:23–24: "Search me, O God, and know my heart; test me and know my anxious thoughts. See if there is any offensive way in me and lead me in the way everlasting."

I would urge you to search your heart and allow God to meet you there, to perform transforming work in you. Take these steps now. Make a commitment to grow by first cultivating that intimacy with God. Then develop a new perspective on your husband. Change those worn-out lenses and learn to relate to him in different and more meaningful ways. Over time you will connect with one another at a much deeper level than you ever thought possible. It's not too late for change, nor is it too late to renew your heart with hope. And remember, it's a hope that God originally intended for you and your husband.

## ABOUT THE AUTHOR

Carrie Oliver has an M.A. in counseling from Denver Seminary and is a licensed professional counselor with PeopleCARE clinics (an affiliate of the Center for Marriage and Family Studies) at John Brown University. Carrie speaks about what women can do to pursue the true, deep intimacy desired with their husband by understanding what leads to good communication, physical intimacy, and close friendship.

VERSES THAT INSPIRE

Your wife shall be like a fruitful vine in the very heart of your house, your children like olive plants all around your table. (Psalm 128:3 NKJV)

Hatred stirs up strife, but love covers all sins. (Proverbs 10:12 NKJV)

Enjoy life with your wife, whom you love. (Ecclesiastes 9:9)

# Beyond Betrayal

LAURIE SHARLENE HALL

*My God, my God, why have you forsaken me?*

—PSALM 22:1

Remember Joseph, the favorite son of Jacob? (You can read this story for yourself in Genesis 37–50.) He had dreams that one day his mother, father, and eleven brothers would bow down to him. This didn't set too well with the brothers. "Who does he think he is, anyway? Bad enough he's daddy's little man—now he wants to lord it over us? Pigs might fly," they groused to each other.

One thing led to another until the brothers decided they would give Little Joe the attitude adjustment he so richly deserved. As the Midianite slave trader was leading Joseph off in shackles, the brothers chortled, "Dream on, Egyptian slave boy!"

Joseph's troubles were just beginning. He was sold on the slave block to a man named Potiphar. After years of faithful service, his master's wife falsely accused him of coming on to her and he was thrown in jail. We don't know how long he was in prison, but we do know that he was thirteen when he was sold into slavery and thirty when he was finally released from prison. That means seventeen years of some kind of misery.

When you read Joseph's story in Genesis, you don't get any sense that he struggled with despair during those seventeen years, but Psalm 105:16–19 (AMP) tells the rest of the story: "Moreover, He [God] called for a famine upon the land of Egypt; He cut off every source of bread. He sent a man before them, even Joseph, who was sold as a servant. His feet they hurt with fetters; he was laid in chains of iron and his soul entered into the iron, until his word . . . came true, until the word of the Lord tried and tested him."

Did you get that? While Joseph was waiting for God's promises to come true, those chains and fetters didn't just cut into his feet and wrists, they cut into his very soul. The cruel iron mockingly reminded him that he was no longer Daddy's darling, no longer the one his family was going to bow and scrape to. No. He was a slave—a man without help or hope. He kept remembering God's word to him and none of what he was going through made any sense.

Finally, seventeen years after the horror show began, he was released from prison so he could interpret Pharaoh's dreams about seven fat cows being devoured by seven emaciated cows and seven plump, juicy ears of corn being devoured by seven withered ears of corn.

"O, Pharaoh, God is letting you know what He's about to do. He's going to send seven years of abundance followed by seven years of famine," Joseph said. "Here's my suggestion: Have a wise administrator gather 20 percent of the seven abundant harvests and store it in granaries. Then, there will be food during the seven lean years."

That interpretation and the accompanying advice didn't

free Joseph from slavery, but it did rocket him into the number two position in the Egyptian government. In that position, Joseph greeted his unsuspecting brothers when they came to him years later and fell on their faces before him, begging for some grain. Turning his back to them, he wept. Suddenly, that long-ago dream made sense. But until this very moment, Joseph never would have guessed it would turn out like this. For seventeen long years, he had clutched his dreams in shackled hands while grappling over the apparent contradiction between God's promises and the reality of his present circumstances. As he stood there on that longed-for day and looked down at his kneeling brothers, Joseph realized that joy burns brightest after hope has entered into the dark agony of despair.

## RISKY BUSINESS

Hope requires us to risk trusting that the dreams God has given us will come true without the foundation of knowing exactly how things will play out or when resolution will occur. Meanwhile, the fetters bruise our feet. The chains cut into our wrists. And our souls enter into the iron.

During those confusing, agonizing years of slavery and imprisonment, Joseph had to keep on keeping on. Keeping on keeping on takes *a lot* of energy. Often, this energy comes to us as we draw on the joy we think we'll experience when our hopes are finally realized. We "pre-experience" this joy as we visualize our hopes being played out a certain way. We close our eyes and imagine how happy we will be when our brothers finally accept us, our marriage is restored, our child is healed, or our job promotion comes through. Our hearts soar over the rainbow as we imagine "someday, somewhere." Refreshed by joy, we dare risk a while longer.

When, despite exhausting ourselves with the effort of it all, we're sold into slavery, the abuse continues, our child dies, or we are given a pinkslip, we come face to face with the fact that our hope. as we have so often visualized it. will never come. Shaken, we now realize that there is no pot of gold at the end of the rainbow for us. Hope dies. Joy withers. And, we enter into despair.

> *This is the great gift of despair: It strips us of that which we think is important in order to awaken us to that which is essential.*

Despair draws a vacuum. In despair, everything that isn't bedrock gets sucked into the abyss. This is the great gift of despair: It strips us of that which we think is important in order to awaken us to that which is essential.

## BEING LEFT IN THE LURCH

In the midst of our despair, we may give lip service to scriptures like Romans 8:28, which tells us that God will work all things together for good for those who love Him, but deep inside our heart we wonder, *If God really loves me, why would He let this happen? Why would He leave me in the lurch? Can I ever trust God again?* Mingled with this enormous sense of having been abandoned by God is the dreadful realization that it is not our enemies who have harmed us, but the ones nearest and dearest to us—the ones we are supposed to be able to count on as being our lifelong intimate allies against what ever harm the world might try to do to us.

Joseph certainly struggled with the bitter pain of betrayal. Betrayal occurs when someone close to us, someone we trust, uses deception and manipulation to get us to participate in our own destruction. Those closest to us know our hearts, they know where we're vulnerable, and they know how to deceive us. They know how to turn all our strengths against us. Our compassion, faithfulness, and desire to love, our talents and abilities, and our naive trust are played against us in a carefully thought-out drama. Meanwhile, we are blissfully unaware that we are being taken to the cleaners because we trust our betrayer.

Betrayal is as old as human history. Caesar's friend Brutus betrayed him to his enemies. Jesus' disciple Judas betrayed Jesus to His enemies—with a *kiss*. Benedict Arnold, a trusted advisor and general in the American Army, conspired to turn West Point over to the British during the Revolutionary War. Arthur Anderson, an accounting firm with a reputation for integrity, covered up the cooked books at WorldCom and Enron, leaving employees without retirement funds and stockholders with devastated portfolios. Meanwhile, Enron executive Ken Lay did a lot of talking about the importance of integrity. He fooled so many people.

## BEING PLAYED FOR THE FOOL

I understand how people can be fooled because I was fooled myself. I met my husband when he was a member of the White House Honor Guard during the Nixon Administration. Son of missionaries, Jack had grown up on the mission field, and when I met him on a blind date, he had a White House security clearance, which meant the FBI had done a thorough background check on him. In my naiveté, I assumed his missionary background and his security clearance vouched for his character. All my family and friends thought he was a super-nice, squeaky-clean guy. I thought I was the luckiest girl in the world.

Shortly after marrying, we left Washington and moved to Texas so my husband could continue school. Soon, he was on the staff of a large church. Everything looked so right, yet I felt there was something wrong. Something I couldn't put my finger on. For one thing, Jack was gone many long hours. When I questioned him about it, he said it was time he needed to serve the Lord. My own father, a very successful businessman, had worked long hours building his business.

My mother had supported him by taking care of things at home. So, while I wasn't happy with Jack's hours, the supportive wife of an absentee husband was a familiar role for me. Even so, I did frequently ask Jack to be home more often. He would always promise me that things would get better after he got this or that project done.

When Jack finally did arrive home, he was too tired, too preoccupied to talk with me or to play with the children. Sometimes, he would just sit and stare. Even on vacation, he was "unavailable." He would get sick the first day of vacation and get well as soon as it was time to go back to work. I was miserable and sought the counsel of my pastor. I was told that I needed to be a more submissive wife and that if I were submissive enough, Jack would become the man that God intended him to be.

So I went to many seminars to learn how to be the perfect Christian wife. I read many marriage books. I attended many Bible studies designed to teach me everything I needed to know to be a godly wife. The information presented in these seminars, Bible studies, and books purported to be scriptural. I was told that God wanted me to be under the covering of my husband's protection and that even if he did something wrong, as long as I stayed under that covering, my children and I would be under God's protection. I wasn't sure how to get under my husband's covering because he didn't seem to me to be doing very much protecting, but I was told that his failings didn't matter. What really mattered was my obedience.

I was strictly warned against rebellion, lest I expose myself to Satan's power. In these teachings rebellion meant not going along with everything your husband wanted you to do. These teachings said that having "a peaceful and gentle spirit" meant you never got angry or felt upset about what was happening in your life. They told me that God required a wife to submit to her husband even if he had proven untrustworthy, simply because wives are required to submit to their husbands. We were told to leave the results to God.

Further, these teachings told me that I had no rights and that having boundaries was a sign of lack of submission. I was told that asking for justice was vindictive and that it was controlling to expect repentance from those who hurt me.

Here I was a young wife, wanting to do her best, and this

is the information I was given about what God required of me. My relationship with God is the essence of my life. I wanted to be who God asked me to be. Yet trying to follow these teachings was bringing death and brokenness into my heart.

I kept searching the Scriptures to see if these teachings were really true. In my book *An Affair of the Mind*, I explore many of these destructive teachings and show how they are not biblical at all. My healing began when the hours of Bible study I was doing showed me that there is a difference between theology and doctrine. Doctrine is what God says about Himself. Theology is man's attempt to interpret God. I was being taught theology while being told it was doctrine. I was told God required me to do things that He didn't require me to do at all. These things were someone else's interpretation of God. You can't live beyond the God you believe in, and if you are told God requires you to participate in behavior that is destructive, you've got no higher court of appeal you can go to.

Jesus asked, "Who do men say that I am?" (Luke 9:18 AMP). In Jesus' day people answered that question many different ways—most of them wrong. That continues to be true today. There's a lot of information and teaching available about what it means to live the Christian life. Yet, a 152-item survey done by George Barna shows there is virtually no difference between the behavior of the "lost" and the behavior of the "saved." In one of the most sickening revelations of our time, it was discovered that the Catholic Church had

*You can't live beyond the God you believe in.*

not only been covering up the sexual abuse of many hundreds of children, it had also enabled and promoted priests who were known pedophiles. Jesus said we will know a tree by its fruits. While there are many good people in the church today, the shocking amount of bad fruit should give us pause to consider whether what we are teaching as Christianity is indeed the truth. "This is eternal life, that they may *know* you, the only true God, and Jesus Christ, whom you have sent" (John 17:3, emphasis mine). Make God right and your whole world changes.

## CHANGE IS INEVITABLE, EXCEPT FROM A VENDING MACHINE.

As I got a more accurate understanding of who God is and the life He calls us to live, I began to change. It was very scary to change because the changes went against everything I had been taught. I wanted to be right with God. So I spent many years agonizing over the things I was coming to understand. Eventually, I gained enough confidence that my new understandings of God were biblically accurate to risk embracing them, no matter what.

Meanwhile, my eyes were being opened more and more to the craziness of my husband's behavior. Through a series of divinely orchestrated events, I discovered that he was lying to me about little things. I was shocked. I never imagined he would lie. What I didn't realize was that he was also lying to me about big things.

Once God began to reveal the lies, my husband started to play a lot of mind games. He would tell me, "Oh, you got that wrong. That's not what I told you. What I told you is . . ." or "Oh, I told you that, you just don't remember." I'd end up feeling like, "How come I can never get anything straight? What's wrong with me?" He would give away my things and not tell me, and I would go looking for them and not be able to find them and think I was going nuts. I would eventually say, "Hey, have you seen my camera?" And he would respond, "Oh, I gave it to Jane." People who play these kinds of mind games are called crazymakers.

Crazymakers discount your reality. The agreements you make with them will be broken and they will act as if you never had that conversation. When you bring it up, you will get a blank look or a "what?" or be told you got it wrong. The schedule you agree upon will be destroyed because crazymakers cannot be counted on and they will wonder why you are so upset. Crazymakers blame you for their mistakes and they will tell you *you* are making *them* crazy.

Crazymakers go to your friends and other family members and tell them you said something unpleasant about them that you never said. They do this because they like to pit people against each other—that gives them a sense of power. Or, they may just make up a story and tell those closest to you that you did something really horrible that you didn't do at all. This strategy works to make people who could be your support system in dealing with the crazymaker think *you* are the one who is causing the problems. The crazymaker will get a lot of sympathy and you will wonder why people are suddenly avoiding you.

## WHEN THE PRINCE YOU'RE KISSING TURNS INTO A FROG

Potiphar's wife was a crazymaker. She told Potiphar that Joseph came on to her to cover up the fact that she came on to him. Joseph's brothers were crazymakers. They told their father, Jacob, that Joseph had been killed by a wild animal to cover up the fact that they had sold him into slavery. Jacob deeply mourned his son. The crazymakers in Joseph's and Jacob's lives caused them a lot of turmoil. That's because in just about every way possible, crazymakers create chaos. They need the chaos to cover up something they don't want you to see.

What my husband didn't want me to see was something he kept very carefully hidden, even from his best friend, who worked with him. My husband had a secret life that had started when he was nineteen. That summer, his parents left him in the States and returned to the mission field. He was a lost, lonely kid who knew he wasn't going to see his family for four years. Shortly after his parents returned to Africa, Jack found a pornographic magazine that had been left at the worksite. He took that magazine back to his hotel room and when he looked at it, he felt the girls in the pictures were smiling right at him. That is the impression pornography tries to create. Suddenly, he didn't feel so lonely.

The problem compounded when he was drafted at the height of the Vietnam War. The unit he was in had to have their hair cut every three days and the barbershop was plastered with centerfolds. Looking at pornography causes endorphins and enkephalins to be released in the brain. These powerful hormones are two hundred times more potent than morphine and more addictive than cocaine. They are a great numbing agent. So looking at those pictures helped Jack feel a little less scared about what was going on in the world around him.

When I met Jack, I had no idea he was looking at

pornography. It wouldn't have occurred to me to ask because he was such a "straight arrow." He kept his pornography usage very secret. In the first twenty years of our marriage, I only saw pornography in the house one time. Even though it was hidden, Jack's pornography usage had a devastating effect on every aspect of our lives.

Eventually, Jack started going to strip shows and hiring prostitutes. All of this was kept very carefully hidden. No one who knew him believed that he would be involved in such deception and perversion. We were all fooled.

When someone you trust has fooled you, it is devastating. You feel stupid and lose the ability to trust yourself. Other people make judgments about you, absolutely sure that they would have had the situation pegged all along. After I wrote *An Affair of the Mind*, I was a guest on a number of radio programs. I received a letter from a listener who told me that she and her husband had been sitting at their kitchen table listening to the show. After the show, she'd turned to her husband and said, "How stupid can she be that she didn't know her husband was into that stuff?" Several weeks later, this woman discovered her husband, a prominent businessman and well-respected Christian leader, was also into that stuff.

Pornography usage is a big problem within the church. According to a 1996 survey of men who attended Promise Keepers stadium events, more than 50 percent of the men attending had been involved with pornography within one week prior to attending the event. The survey was repeated the next year with similar results. Another study found that 51 percent of married Christian men surveyed were masturbating to pornography. According to Robert T. Michael's book *Sex in America: A Definitive Survey*, 41 percent of all men (including conservative Protestants) and 16 percent of all women reported having done one or more of the following in the previous twelve months: watching an X-rated movie, visiting a club with nude or seminude dancers, purchasing sexually explicit books, magazines, erotic devices or sex toys, or calling a sex phone number.

Through a series of answered prayers, God revealed my husband's secret life. I will never forget the day I found out. I was destroyed. Initially, my husband said he wanted to deal with his addiction. He begged for a chance to save the marriage and went into therapy. I went with him. The next few years were the most difficult times of my life. One counselor told me I just needed to get over it and support my husband in his recovery. Another gave me a series of videos on sex and told me I just needed to be more responsive. This counselor had no idea that one of the aspects of sexual addiction is that the addict withholds sex from the spouse. It is not the other way around. I have listened to so many women weep as they talked about how people assumed their husbands became involved with pornography because they were frigid. Nothing could have been further from the truth.

Another counselor told me the reason my husband lied to me was that I was too demanding. At that very moment, my husband was lying to him. When I told the counselor what was going on, he expressed shock and said, "Jack wouldn't lie to *me*." Yes, he would. He was lying to everyone, especially himself.

After two years of these games, we were separated for nine months. During this time, Jack began to deal with his addiction. At the end of the nine months, he came home. He had begun to deal with his problem but he hadn't healed, and we limped along for several more years. Jack finally found a counselor who could help him. There were some very bright moments during the next few years when I thought we were going to make it.

Then, there was a marked personality change and everything started going downhill. Things went from bad to worse to very bad. In the end, I was quite frightened of my husband. That was new. Until the last few years, the dysfunction had been crazymaking but not frightening. When it became frightening, I knew I had to leave, and I did.

That decision cost me a lot. I lost family. I lost friends. I lost ministry opportunities. The beautiful home that I loved so much was sold. I left behind most of my belongings. I lost the whole world and gained my soul.

## HE PLACES THE SOLITARY IN FAMILIES

I spent most of the first year after my marriage ended in shell shock. My moods were all over the planet. I was enormously thankful to have escaped alive. I was devastated that my husband had chosen his addiction over the marriage. I was amazed at the deep peace I felt. I was frightened about how I would provide for myself. I spent much of that first year in Sherbrooke, Quebec, as a guest of Carrefour Chretien de l'Estrie, a church I had spoken at the previous year. When everything went south, I called Pastor Daniel and he said, "Come up." I did. What a gift those people were to me.

One Sunday morning shortly after I arrived in Quebec, I was feeling so sad. Here I was in another country with people I could not understand because I didn't speak the language. I had just lost my mother and father. I had few possessions. I had lost my home. I had lost my marriage. I felt cut off and so alone. I cried out to the Lord, praying from Psalm 68:5–6: "A Father to the fatherless and a judge and protector of the widow is God in His holy habitation. God places the solitary in families and gives the desolate a home in which to dwell; He leads the prisoners out into prosperity."

Later that morning I went to church, and after the service I spoke to Nadine, one of the few bilingual people in the congregation. Even though we hadn't spent much time together, I felt a very special bond with Nadine and she felt the same for me. I told Nadine that my family had originally come from Quebec. My French Canadian great-grandfather was a young man when his father was killed. His mother, unable to care for so many children, had sent him to the States. He never went back. My family knew very little about his background and we never explored our French connections. We had never even been to Canada.

Nadine asked me what my maiden name was and I told her. Suppressing a smile, she asked if I would be back for the evening service. That night, Nadine came with a copy of her family genealogy. We were cousins. God had put this homeless, fatherless, motherless, husbandless orphan in a family she never knew she had.

Within a year on very little money, I had a wonderfully comfortable bed, new silverware and plates, new sheets and towels, and a terrific sofa. My housemate, Dyane, had been through many of the same experiences I had. We often marveled at how similar our stories were. She was such a comfort to me. Within two years, I moved into my own apartment. Within three years, I had begun to build a new community of supportive friends. Along the way, there have been many days of joy and peace; there have also been days of over-whelm and sheer terror. No matter what the day has brought, God's grace and provision met me there.

## DO YOU WANT THAT TOASTED OR PLAIN?

Joseph's story reminds us that when people we trust deceive us, we are force-fed the bitter bread of betrayal. Perhaps you've been served a slice from this loaf. My recollection is that it doesn't come with jam, or even a decent amount of butter—absolutely nothing to help it slide down your throat before it lands like a bomb in your belly. I don't think you even get to choose if you want white or whole wheat. Nope, someone just rips off a slab and flings it your way.

Perhaps that someone was a spouse who walked into the living room one night after you'd done the dishes for the ten thousandth time in your life together and announced he wanted a divorce because he'd met someone on-line. And here you were thinking about how you need to make the sale at Wal-Mart so the kids can get their new school clothes, or how you need to change the oil before next month's vacation, and you didn't even have any idea that Christmas stockings and children's giggles could be stolen in cyberspace.

Or maybe your slice got served as a nurse tightened the tourniquet around your arm so she could do an AIDS test because your husband announced he'd been sleeping around. And there, all wrapped up in tissue paper and buried in the bottom of your grandmother's cedar chest, is the nightgown you wore on your wedding night. And the ribbons haven't faded and the tucks in the bodice are still as crisp and delicate as they were twenty-five years ago when you gave yourself to the only one you've ever given yourself to—only now there's a horrible stain where the bread landed.

Or perhaps the slab is hurled as you sit, squirming, before your church's board of elders, asking them to help you save your marriage because you've just discovered your husband is involved with pornography and prostitutes, and the elders look you in the eye and tell you he wouldn't have had to resort to glossy pretties if you were a better wife. He's so weak because you're so strong, they tell you. And by the way, you're an unsubmissive wife if you don't sleep with him because you're afraid of getting a sexually transmitted disease. And about that time he pushed you into the living room wall—what did you do to provoke him, anyway? Meanwhile, all the chicken pies you baked and all the times you washed his underwear and all the times you caught your breath when you looked at him because even after twenty years of marriage the sight of him still turned you on, count for nothing.

The thing about betrayal is that it sort of sneaks up on you and sucks out your hope. There you are enjoying lamb chops with your brothers, but one of them has really got it in for you and as you pass him the rolls, he looks you in the eyes and says to himself, *He'll never know what hit him.* The next thing you know, you're looking at the back end of a camel on your way to Egypt. It's the profound cruelty and the utter rejection of all you are by those who should know and love you best that makes betrayal so very, very galling. Meanwhile, there's this ugly twist to this loaf—you don't get served this bread because you've done something wrong, but because you've done something very, very right.

Joseph's betrayal had its foundation not in his guilt, but in his righteousness. His decision to stay out of someone else's marriage bed enraged the lust of Potiphar's wife. She took vengeance by having him thrown in prison.

## BEING OUR OWN WORST ENEMY

The worst thing about betrayal is that in betrayal, all our strengths are turned against us. For example, it's a strength to love. Our ability to love others is life-giving to them. Our ability to love also lets us know when others are treating us in loving ways and when they are treating us in abusive ways. However, our ability to love tempts us. Should we turn the other cheek? Or should we shake the dust off our feet and move on? What if, as we chose to work through deep betrayals of trust by giving time to see if our relationship with the one who wounded us can be healed, we are abandoned by others who judge us as codependents who love too much? What if we actually do abandon ourselves to codependent confusion by merely loving to be loved? What if, after putting much energy into reconciliation, we are forced to abandon hope for the relationship because the other person doesn't want to work things out?

It's a strength to have faith that God hears and answers prayer. Our faith in God causes us to boldly come before the throne and intercede for the needs of the world. Our faith also causes us to persevere in prayer for those who despitefully use us and therefore need our forgiveness. However, our faith tempts us. Does God's delay in answering mean I have hidden sin that needs to be confessed? How many years does He expect me to pray about this, anyway? What is my part and what is His part and what is the other person's part?

What if faith asks me to abandon my hope because God's answer to my fervent prayers is, "No. I have another plan." If God says no to something that's really, really important to me, does that mean He doesn't love me? How do I handle misguided friends who continue to urge me to pray for God to "fix" my situation when it is clearly unwise to stay any longer in the craziness?

When someone uses our strengths to set us up to be taken to the cleaners, we are placed in a situation where, in order to save ourselves from harm, we must choose to slay our own strengths. This is evil doing its best to kill our spirit.

## LEAD US NOT INTO TEMPTATION

In Dietrich Bonhoeffer's *Creation and Fall,* he said:

> The temptation of which the whole Bible speaks does not have to do with the testing of my strength, for it is of the very essence of temptation in the Bible that all my strength—to my horror, and without my being able to do anything about it—is turned against me; really all my powers, including my good and pious powers, fall into the hands of the enemy power and are now led into the field against me. Before there can be any testing of my powers, I have been robbed of them.
>
> This is the decisive fact in the temptation of the Christian, that he is abandoned, abandoned by all his powers—indeed, attacked by them—abandoned by all men, abandoned by God himself. His heart shakes, and has fallen into complete darkness. He himself is nothing. The enemy is everything. God has taken his hand away from him. He has left him for a little while (Isa 54:7). The man is alone in his temptation. Nothing stands by him. For a little

while the devil has room. The hardest and highest temptation and suffering that God sometimes attacks and exercises his greatest saints with is when the heart of man feels nothing less than that God has abandoned him with his grace. . . .

So here's the real test of the school of betrayal: What will you do and who will you be in the midst of your betrayal? What will you do and who will you be when all your strengths are turned against you? Will you slay the best parts of yourself to avoid further trouble? Or will you suffer the trouble and hold true to who you are?

While Joseph was stepping around camel dung on his way to the Egyptian slave block, he had to grapple with whether he was going to give up or be the best he could be in a terrible situation. When Potiphar's wife came on to him, he had to decide whether he would comfort himself in his misery by indulging in sexual pleasure (after all, he was just a good red-blooded Jewish boy and everybody else was doing it) or remember that he was the kind of man of who didn't take that which didn't belong to him.

During those long prison nights, fellow inmates could hear Joe mumbling to himself, "Let 'em rot! They deserve it!" Then they would hear him flop over on that hard slab of wood he called a bed and whisper, "But, if I treat them like they've treated me, I lose myself. God, if You're up there anywhere, help me!" Finally, years later, when his brothers came begging bread, Joseph looked long and hard into their eyes and wondered, "Do I feed them to the sharks, or do I invite them to the banqueting table?"

While he was helpless to stop others from betraying him, at every decision point, Joseph chose not to betray himself. Instead, he held onto who he was. No matter what others said about him, and no matter what others did to him, Joseph knew who he was and he acted accordingly. Joseph was a man of integrity.

## DELIVER US FROM EVIL

Crazymakers give us crazy, mixed-up messages about who we really are. If we believe those messages, we will make choices that will betray our highest and best self. Life is all about the choices we make. The choices I have made in the past have led me to where I am today. The choices I make today will lead me to where I will be tomorrow. My tomorrow is full of promise and that promise starts with who I am today. So a big part of my recovery from betrayal has been to remember who I am and live accordingly.

As part of living a life true to myself, I've worked on getting clear about what my boundaries are. Boundaries are "nos." They are what I will not allow others to do to me. I've also worked to get clear about what I require of others in their interactions with me and I've learned how to make my requests so that I am heard. I've taken a hard look at the things I tolerate and am working on becoming a toleration-free zone. Finally, I know what my needs are and I take responsibility to see that they get met. I have moved from suffering from the effects of someone else's bad choices to being at cause for my own life. And it feels so extraordinarily great!

So, while losing everything at fifty is not a happy circumstance, I have chosen to look at this turning point as an amazing gift rather than a terrible tragedy. I have an opportunity to start all over and create a life I really love. I create that life as I make the choice to live in the present, for the present is all I really have. The past is over and the future is not yet. I just have today. I just have this moment, and this moment has everything I need. It is full beyond measure with gifts of all sorts. That is why it is called *the present*.

I was regretting the past and fearing the future.

Suddenly, my Lord was speaking.

My name is I AM.

He paused.

I waited.

He continued.

When you live in the past with its mistakes and regrets,

it is hard. I am not there.

My name is not I WAS.

When you live in the future with its problems and fears,

it is hard. I am not there.

My name is not I WILL BE.

When you live in this moment, it is not hard. I am here.

My name is I AM.

HELEN MALLICOAT

## ABOUT THE AUTHOR

Laurie Sharlene Hall graduated *summa cum laude* with a Ph.D. from the School of Hard Knocks, which is the most expensive university in the world. Her dissertation was a groundbreaking book called *An Affair of the Mind*, which explores the effects pornography has on a marriage. A guest on over two hundred radio and TV programs, Laurie is one of the few women ever to address a Promise Keepers arena event. A professional coach, Laurie works with people who want to rebuild their personal foundations and create lives they really, Really, REALLY love.

## VERSES THAT INSPIRE

If any of you lacks wisdom, he should ask God,
who gives generously to all without finding fault,
and it will be given to him. (James 1:5)

One thing I ask of the LORD, this is what I seek: that I may dwell in the house of the LORD all the days of my life, to gaze upon the beauty of the LORD and to seek him in his temple. (Psalm 27:4)

He was in the world, and though the world was made through him, the world did not recognize him. He came to that which was his own, but his own did not receive him. Yet to all who received him, to those who believed in his name, he gave the right to become children of God.
(John 1:10–12)

"Sing, O barren woman,
   you who never bore a child;
burst into song, shout for joy,
   you who were never in labor;
because more are the children of the
   desolate woman
   than of her who has a husband,"

                                        says the LORD.

"Enlarge the place of your tent,

stretch your tent curtains wide,

do not hold back;

lengthen your cords,

strengthen your stakes.

For you will spread out to the right and to the left;

your descendants will dispossess nations

and settle in their desolate cities.


"Do not be afraid; you will not suffer shame.

Do not fear disgrace; you will not be

humiliated.

You will forget the shame of your youth

and remember no more the reproach of your

widowhood." (Isaiah 54:1–4)

Extraordinary Women (EWomen), a ministry of the American Association of Christian Counselors (AACC), is a faith-based movement focused on taking women closer to the heart of God. For more information on our dynamic training programs, conferences, resources, and membership benefits, visit *Ewomen.net* or call 1-800-526-8673 or write P.O. Box 739, Forest, VA 24551.

AACC is a membership organization of more than 50,0000 clinical, pastoral, and lay counselors dedicated to promoting excellence in faith-based counseling. Post Office Box 739, Forest, VA 24551; 1-800-526-8673; *www.aacc.net*

*Shine* Magazine is a centerpiece publication for Extraordinary Women. *Shine* bridges the gap between a woman's outer and inner beauty. Each issue celebrates the spiritual, intellectual, and physical aspects of womanhood. Isaiah 60:1 "Arise, SHINE, for your light has come, and the glory of the LORD rises upon you."